Improving Thinking About Thinking in the Classroom

What are the best ways to enhance metacognition in the course of classroom teaching? This research-to-practice book shows how to go beyond simple student reflection to use any of 19 different practical strategies. Each chapter describes a different method, gives the research evidence to support the effectiveness of the method and then provides guidelines for implementation. You will learn about programs within traditional curriculum subjects, programs across the traditional curriculum, programs focusing especially on self-regulation, programs for disabled and special needs students, and programs embedded in a digital environment. You will also discover common features of the methods, so you can see the similarities across the methods and ultimately devise your own ways to develop metacognition and self-regulated learning. With the powerful practices in this book, students will develop a refined ability to think about how they think and learn, preparing them for their futures beyond school.

Keith J. Topping is a researcher, educator, author and international speaker. His special interests are peer learning, parents as educators, social competence, computer-assisted assessment and inclusion. Topping has written 29 books and over 400 other publications including over 200 peer-reviewed journal papers.

Also Available from Routledge Eye On Education
(routledge.com/k-12)

Improving Thinking in the Classroom: What Works for Enhancing Cognition
Keith J. Topping

Improving Reading Comprehension of Self-Chosen Books through Computer Assessment and Feedback: Best Practices from Research
Keith J. Topping

The Student Motivation Handbook: 50 Ways to Boost an Intrinsic Desire to Learn
Larry Ferlazzo

Passionate Learners, 3rd Edition: How to Engage and Empower Your Students
Pernille Ripp

Rigor Is Not a Four-Letter Word, 3rd Edition
Barbara R. Blackburn

Improving Thinking About Thinking in the Classroom
What Works for Enhancing Metacognition

Keith J. Topping

Routledge
Taylor & Francis Group
NEW YORK AND LONDON

Designed cover image: © Getty Images

First published 2024
by Routledge
605 Third Avenue, New York, NY 10158

and by Routledge
4 Park Square, Milton Park, Abingdon, Oxon, OX14 4RN

Routledge is an imprint of the Taylor & Francis Group, an informa business

© 2024 Keith J. Topping

The right of Keith J. Topping to be identified as author of this work has been asserted in accordance with sections 77 and 78 of the Copyright, Designs and Patents Act 1988.

All rights reserved. No part of this book may be reprinted or reproduced or utilized in any form or by any electronic, mechanical, or other means, now known or hereafter invented, including photocopying and recording, or in any information storage or retrieval system, without permission in writing from the publishers.

Trademark notice: Product or corporate names may be trademarks or registered trademarks, and are used only for identification and explanation without intent to infringe.

Library of Congress Cataloging-in-Publication Data
Names: Topping, Keith J., author.
Title: Improving thinking about thinking in the classroom : what works for enhancing metacognition / Keith J. Topping.
Description: New York, NY : Routledge, 2024. | Includes bibliographical references.
Identifiers: LCCN 2023055575 (print) | LCCN 2023055576 (ebook) | ISBN 9781032512952 (paperback) | ISBN 9781032514338 (hardback) | ISBN 9781003402190 (ebook)
Subjects: LCSH: Thought and thinking--Study and teaching. | Cognitive learning. | Metacognition.
Classification: LCC LB1590.3 .T669 2024 (print) | LCC LB1590.3 (ebook) | DDC 370.15/2--dc23/eng/20231214
LC record available at https://lccn.loc.gov/2023055575
LC ebook record available at https://lccn.loc.gov/2023055576

ISBN: 978-1-032-51433-8 (hbk)
ISBN: 978-1-032-51295-2 (pbk)
ISBN: 978-1-003-40219-0 (ebk)

DOI: 10.4324/9781003402190

Typeset in Palatino
by SPi Technologies India Pvt Ltd (Straive)

Contents

1 Introduction 1

SECTION A   Programs Within Particular Traditional Subjects 13

2 Science 15

3 Mathematics 24

4 Language, Reading and Writing 32

SECTION B   Methods Across the Traditional Curriculum 43

5 Dialog and Think-Aloud 45

6 Questioning 55

7 Summarizing 65

8 Modeling 76

9 Predictions 87

10 Visualization 97

11 Diagrams 111

12 Mnemonics 119

13 Self-Assessment 127

14 Peer Assessment 138

**SECTION C   Programs Focusing Especially on
Self-Regulated Learning 149**

15 Metacognition and Decision Making 151

16 Self-Regulation and Metacognitive Skills 162

**SECTION D   Programs Focusing Especially on
Memory and Disability 185**

17 Metacognition and Memory 187

18 Metacognition, Memory and Disability 194

**SECTION E   Programs Embedded in Digital
Technology 203**

19 Computerized and Online Learning 205

20 Metacognition and Artificial Intelligence 216

SECTION F   Discussion and Conclusion 231

21 Discussion and Conclusion 233

1

Introduction

The aim of this book is to help school teachers improve the thinking skills, metacognition and self-regulated learning of their students/pupils, not just in a narrowly focused area but across the curriculum and beyond it, with a view to preparing them for the world beyond education. Long after they have forgotten the detailed knowledge they were taught, the students' refined and widely applicable ability to think and think about their thinking should help them perform better in a job or profession and help them solve everyday problems in their personal life, leading to a happier person with a greater sense of well-being.

This book is one of a pair published more or less at the same time with closely related themes. After definition of the terms, both books draw on research evidence for the effectiveness of the various methods suggested. Then implementation guidelines are given to teachers, before the common threads of the methods are drawn together in a discussion and conclusion. The first book was called "Improving Thinking in the Classroom: What Works for Enhancing Cognition". This second book is called "Improving Thinking About Thinking in the Classroom: What Works for Enhancing Metacognition". The first book was about matters that teachers consider quite frequently. The second is about matters that teachers consider less frequently. But what exactly is metacognition and, beyond this, self-regulated learning?

Definition

The *Oxford English Dictionary* defines metacognition as "awareness and understanding of one's own thought processes". Similarly, Wikipedia suggests that metacognition is an awareness of one's thought processes and an understanding of the patterns behind them.

Metacognition was first conceptualized by Flavell (1976). Flavell defined metacognition as knowledge about cognition *and* control of cognition. It could be defined as awareness and understanding of one's own thought processes and involves knowing your strengths and weaknesses as a learner, but beyond this, it involves the ability to control one's own thinking, a process now known as self-regulation.

Perkins and Salomon (1992) distinguished four types of metacognition: tacit, aware, strategic and reflective. Tacit learners are unaware of their metacognitive knowledge but might do metacognition implicitly. Aware learners consciously know about some of the kinds of thinking that they do, but their thinking is not necessarily deliberate or planned. Strategic learners organize their thinking by using (for example) problem solving, grouping and classifying, evidence seeking, decision making, and so on. Reflective learners are not only strategic, but also reflect upon their learning whilst it is happening, considering the success or otherwise of any strategies used and then revising them as appropriate. Obviously, the aim of the teachers is to raise metacognition in any student in any subject up through these four categories.

Self-regulated learning (SRL) is the ability to understand and consequently manage your thinking, leading to more effective learning (Zimmerman & Schunk, 2001). This is the strategic active outcome of metacognition – the application of metacognitive awareness to action in the real world – but it obviously requires motivation to drive it. Self-regulated learners tend to believe that intelligence is learned and can be changed (as opposed to fixed views of intelligence) and attribute their successes or failures to factors within their control (e.g., effort expended on a task or effective use of strategies), not to innate ability. Self-regulation is a cyclical process wherein learners regulate their learning in three phases: the forethought phase (i.e., processes that precede the learning act), the performance phase (i.e., processes during the learning act) and the self-reflection phase (i.e., processes after the learning act).

Audience

The primary audience for this book is preservice and in-service school teachers as well as teacher educators and individuals involved in supporting the ongoing professional development of educators, in both elementary (primary) education and secondary (middle and high school) education. In addition, school principals, district superintendents and managers will seek to use the book as a reference source. Officials in local and national government are also likely to use the book, as will researchers. Generally, mention of tertiary (college and university) education has been avoided.

Zitzmann et al. (2023) speak to the importance of having findings from research in educational psychology communicated to teachers, schools, school authorities, or policy makers. They comment: "Any practical recommendations should be preceded by a summary of findings, which should be meaningful to stakeholders and be communicated in such a way that these persons will easily understand them" (p. 2). Effect sizes are useful, but are a form of average and do not relate to any individual student with whom the teacher may be especially concerned.

Why Read This Book?

The book is intended to give the evidence base for metacognitive programs and methods in an easy and comprehensible way. This should reassure teachers and their managers that teaching practice is well substantiated. It also gives details of how each method can be implemented, and refers readers to the original texts for more detail. Thus, readers are reassured that these methods work, and are also given information about how to practically implement them in the classroom.

Search Methods

Five relevant research databases (ERIC, JSTOR, Scopus, Web of Science and Google Scholar) were searched for peer-reviewed journal papers using the terms "metacognition" *or* "self-regulated learning" *or* "self regulated learning" *and* (the title of the chapter). Consideration was given to adding "school" to this list, but many papers did not have school in the title, keywords or abstract even if they were based in school, so this keyword was omitted and papers about college and university excluded manually. In the case of many chapters, additional search terms were added. Beyond this, other sources which compiled relevant research papers were searched manually, such as the journal *Metacognition and Learning*. Masters and doctoral theses were excluded, as their quality was so various. Chapters in books and books were also excluded on the grounds that they had not been peer reviewed.

Structure of the Book

Many books which claim to be evidence-based just give vague background research which is often not reflected in the recommendations they make, but in the case of this book the research cited is specifically about the method which is described.

The chapters (apart from this first and the last one) are divided into five sections. Section A describes programs and methods relevant to specific subjects already operating in the traditional curriculum. Section B describes methods operable across the traditional curriculum. Section C describes programs focusing especially on self-regulated learning. Section D describes programs for disabled or special needs students. Section E describes programs embedded in digital environments. This means that teachers heavily restricted by traditional curriculum requirements can still find ways described here to introduce metacognitive skills, including those which go beyond awareness into behavior change. Further, the methods can be applied in digital environments with or without students with special needs, reflecting modern tendencies to intervene online where possible and an important aspect of inclusivity.

In all these sections, the chapters follow a similar model: first the area of interest is defined if necessary (especially in Section B), then the relevant research is summarized by way of Background, then a Specific Program is chosen as an example and its evidence summarized, then its implementation is addressed (including assessment of outcomes if this is mentioned), and the chapter ends with a (short) list of references and a bibliography for those who wish to read further.

The final chapter "Discussion and Conclusion" draws together common features of the methods, so teachers can see the commonalities across the methods. This should help them to devise their own methods for developing metacognition and self-regulated learning.

The book thus offers a summary of the independent, peer-reviewed research evidence on the methods described. This should address many of the major concerns of schools, who will have questions like: "Does it work?", "How should it be implemented to make it work?" and "Is it cheaper and more efficient in teacher time than what we were doing before?" This review of evidence should thus reassure schools that their practice is evidence-based and well substantiated, lead them to improve their implementation of such programs, and enable them to state and defend their case in that regard to school district leaders, managers, local and national government, parents and other stakeholders. It will also be of interest to researchers, especially in areas where data are sparser or more difficult to track.

How to Read This Book

Hopefully, the book is not too long for the busy teacher to find time to read at least some of it. Obviously, this introductory chapter should be read first. After that, consider your context – how restricted are you in terms of the time available and the willingness of your hierarchy to allow some innovation? If neither of these are positive, you might need to be subtle about how you introduce metacognitive activity. Section A methods can be done within a timetabled existing subject, and so are relatively easy to smuggle in. Section B methods are easily smuggled in, because you can try each one at a time without undue time consumption. These first two sections are probably the ones to concentrate on.

Section C methods are going to take more preparation, not least as you might feel less certain initially about what you are doing, but again can operate within the traditional curriculum. Section D focuses on students with disability and special needs, so if you don't have any such students, you can certainly skip this section for now. Section E is about the digital environment and is perhaps more futuristic than the other sections. If you have good technology support you might well be interested in this section, but if not, you might want to skip it for now.

The last chapter tries to draw together the threads of commonality from all the previous sections, and may be useful for principals and school leaders or managers to read after they have read the Introduction. It should also be useful for class teachers, since it will help you see what are the common elements or patterns across all these methods – i.e., increase your metacognition.

Statistical Analysis

Some (but not many) statistics are present in what follows, so here is a brief overview. The *number* of observations is usually indicated as n or N (this is important in terms of the size and consequently significance of the study). The arithmetic *mean* or *average* is the sum of all observations divided by the number of observations. The *standard deviation* (s.d.) is a measure of the amount of variance in the data. The correlation between two different variables is often expressed as a *correlation coefficient* (*r*), which indicates on a scale from -1 through 0 to +1 whether the relationship is negative or positive and its degree.

In some analyses you will see that the difference between sets of observations is tested for statistical significance. One way of doing this is with the *t-test*, which compares the means with reference to their s.d.s and ns and sees if the value of the resulting statistic *t* is large enough to be statistically significant. Other ways are more complicated to explain.

Statistical significance (p) is a quantification of whether what you see is likely just due to random chance, or whether it is more probably the result of some influential factor you are studying. Usually, a criterion of probability of 0.05 or 5% is set as the limit of statistical significance, below which what you see is more likely due to your factor of interest, and above which it is more likely due to random chance. Sometimes the sample size (n) for an analysis is very large and one result of this is that even very small differences appear statistically significant, as statistical significance is strongly affected by sample size – the larger the sample, the more likely statistical significance becomes.

An alternative way of looking at this is via *effect size* (ES) (a quantitative measure of the magnitude of effect). The larger the ES, the stronger the relationship between two variables. ESs are often approximately categorized according to their size: Very Small = 0.01, Small = 0.20, Medium = 0.50, Large = 0.80, Very Large = 1.20, Huge = 2.00. There is another kind of effect size (eta-squared or η^2) used occasionally, which we will talk about when it occurs.

Terminology

Bearing in mind differences in nomenclature and terms between the USA and the UK (among other countries), the book is written in trans-Atlantic language, giving synonyms wherever appropriate (e.g., elementary/primary, students/pupils, mathematics not math or maths). Where single terms are used, the US version is usually given.

What Do Teachers Think About Metacognition?

There are a number of studies of teacher perceptions of thinking skills and metacognition. Generally, they suggest that teachers have a vague perception that thinking skills and metacognition are a good idea, but little idea about how to develop them. This is true irrespective of the country involved. Of course, that is why this book has been written.

Metacognitive strategies are rare in ordinary teaching (Ellis et al., 2014). They are rarely mentioned in curriculum documents and appear very patchily across the curriculum or from year to year. Classroom assessments also influence the degree of metacognition – if metacognition is not required in the final assessment, what is the motivation to use it? Further, are assessment questions convergent (only looking for one right answer) or divergent (accommodating various points of view)?

Kistner et al. (2015) found that, on average, teachers taught metacognitive strategies through implicit instruction as compared to explicit instruction at a ratio of 5 to 1, i.e., they modeled it without explaining how the strategy might be effective. Alternatively, modeling while simultaneously verbalizing one's thought processes or asking targeted questions during the demonstration is a form of explicit strategy instruction. Explicit strategy instruction is positively correlated with achievement gains, while using an implicit method is less so. Characteristics of explicit strategy instruction include modeling, explaining the benefits of using the strategy, and providing repeated opportunities for using the strategy in guided and independent practice formats.

Overviews of Effectiveness of Metacognition – Does It Work?

Given this, do these programs work? There is certainly a strong general effect of metacognitive training on overall attainment. Effect sizes (ESs) in meta-analyses vary from 0.69 (Dignath & Büttner, 2008) to 0.55 (Eberhart et al., 2023) – moderate to large. Turning to subject disciplines, Donker et al. (2014) found ESs of 1.25 for writing, 0.73 for science, 0.66 for mathematics and 0.36

for reading. This study found no differences in effectiveness according to students' ability levels. De Boer et al. (2018) found ESs of 0.50 at post-test, but 0.63 at follow-up.

More recently, Muijs and Bokhove (2020) conducted an evidence review of metacognition and self-regulation, noting that, on average, intelligence uniquely accounted for 10% of variance in learning, metacognitive skills uniquely accounted for 17% of the variance, whereas both predictors together shared another 20% of variance in learning. There was some evidence that metacognitive training could aid students with learning difficulties and behavioral disorders (e.g., Losinski et al., 2014). Longitudinal and follow-up studies from various countries all showed positive long-term gains. There was some evidence that developing teachers' own metacognition and SRL had a positive impact on pupil attainment.

Even more recently, Eberhart et al. (2023) conducted a meta-analysis of metacognition in elementary aged children. Only two databases were searched and 810 publications narrowed to 44 papers, 53 studies, minimum sample size n = 10. Of 131 effect sizes, the effect size for mathematics was 0.60 and for other academic subjects 0.55, while the effect size for metacognition outcomes was 0.34. Sixteen studies had some follow-up (average 15 weeks), with effect size 0.29. Self-efficacy also showed improvement (ES = 0.24). Metacognition interventions were more effective for older elementary students. They were also more effective when delivered by teachers rather than researchers. Number of sessions (intensity) was not a significant factor. Some direct instruction and modeling gave increased effect sizes and 81% of the studies included some practice. ESs were greater (0.53) when they resulted from researcher-developed tests than from standardized tests (0.19). So, yes, metacognition works, but variably according to context.

Assessment

A major issue for teachers is that, even assuming that instruction and engagement with metacognition has happened in the classroom, how do you know that it is having any effect? Of course, if student achievement increases compared to non-participants, that is good, but how do you know that metacognition made the difference?

Dinsmore et al. (2008), in their overview, found a range of measures used to study metacognition and SRL: self-report, observation, think-aloud, interviews, performance ratings and diaries. A meta-analysis of self-monitoring as an integral part of self-regulated learning was conducted by Dignath et al. (2023). Tools that notionally fostered learners' monitoring, such as learning journals, portfolios, or rubrics, were supposed to promote self-regulation and improve performance, and this analysis examined their effectiveness on academic achievement, self-regulated learning and motivation. Included studies numbered 32, yielding 109 effect sizes from 3492 participants.

There was a moderate effect size on academic achievement (d = 0.42), but lower effects on self-regulated learning (d = 0.19) and motivation (d = 0.17), moderated by characteristics of the tool and implementation quality. Effect sizes were highest for tools that (1) focused on the monitoring of both learning content as well as learning behavior, (2) stimulated metacognitive monitoring, and (3) were implemented in shorter studies. Higher effects were found for monitoring interventions that included teacher feedback and allowed learners to revise their work based on this feedback.

What This Book Is Not

The approaches mentioned in the chapters that follow have been found to be effective, and the research on them is briefly summarized. However, there are many other thinking and metacognition programs and methods which have not been widely evaluated or evaluated at all. We do not mention these approaches further in this book.

Now we will turn to the major chapters in this book, which examine individual approaches more carefully and spell out the implementation issues, starting in Section A with programs which are embedded in particular subjects.

References

de Boer, H., Donker, A. S., Kostons, D. D. N. M., & van der Werf, G. P. C. (2018). Long-term effects of metacognitive strategy instruction on student academic performance: A meta-analysis. *Educational Research Review*, *24*, 98–115. https://doi.org/10.1016/j.edurev.2018.03.002

Dignath, C., & Büttner, G. (2008). Components of fostering self-regulated learning among students. A meta-analysis on intervention studies at primary and secondary school level. *Metacognition and Learning*, *3*, 231–264. doi: 10.1007/s11409-008-9029-x

Dignath, C., van Ewijk, R., Perels, F., & Fabriz, S. (2023). Let learners monitor the learning content and their learning behavior! A meta-analysis on the effectiveness of tools to foster monitoring. *Educational Psychology Review*, *35*, 62. https://doi.org/10.1007/s10648-023-09718-4

Dinsmore, D., Alexander, P., & Loughlin, S. (2008). Focusing the conceptual lens on metacognition, self-regulation, and self-regulated learning. *Educational Psychology Review*, *20*(4), 391–409. doi: 10.1007/s10648-008-9083-6

Donker, A. S., de Boer, H., Kostons, D., Dignath van Ewijk, C. C., & van der Werf, M. P. C. (2014). Effectiveness of learning strategy instruction on academic performance: A meta-analysis. *Educational Research Review*, *11*, 1–26. https://doi.org/10.1016/j.edurev.2013.11.002

Eberhart, J., Schäfer, F., & Bryce, D. (2023). Are metacognition interventions in school-aged children effective? Evidence from a series of meta-analyses. *PsyArXiv Preprints*. https://doi.org/10.31234/osf.io/475br or https://psyarxiv.com/475br/

Ellis, A. K., Denton, D. W., & Bond, J. B. (2014). An analysis of research on metacognitive teaching strategies. *Procedia – Social and Behavioral Sciences*, *116*, 4015–4024. doi: 10.1016/j.sbspro.2014.01.883

Flavell, J. H. (1976). Metacognitive aspects of problem solving. In L. B. Resnick (Ed.), *The Nature of Intelligence* (pp. 231–236). Hillsdale, NJ: Erlbaum.

Kistner, S., Rakoczy, K., Otto, B., Klieme, E., & Büttner, G. (2015). Teaching learning strategies: The role of instructional context and teacher beliefs. *Journal for Educational Research Online*, *7*(1), 176–197. doi: urn:nbn:de:0111-pedocs-110527

Losinski, M., Cuenca-Carlino, Y., Zablocki, M., & Teagarden, J. (2014). Examining the efficacy of self-regulated strategy development for students with emotional or behavioral disorders: A meta-analysis. *Behavioral Disorders*, *40*(1), 51–67. https://doi.org/10.17988/0198-7429-40.1.52

Muijs, D., & Bokhove, C. (2020). *Metacognition and Self-Regulation: Evidence Review*. London: Education Endowment Foundation. https://educationendowmentfoundation.org.uk/evidence-summaries/evidence-reviews/metacognition-and-self-regulation-review

Perkins, D. N., & Salomon, G. (1992). Transfer of learning. In T. Husten (Ed.), *International Encyclopedia of Education*, 2nd edition, *2*, 6452–6457. Oxford: Pergamon Press.

Zimmerman, B. J., & Schunk, D. H. (Eds.) (2001). *Self-Regulated Learning and Academic Achievement: Theoretical Perspectives*, 2nd edition. New York and London: Routledge.

Zitzmann, S., Machts, N., Hübner, N., Schauber, S., Möller, J., & Lindner, C. (2023). The yet underestimated importance of communicating findings from educational trials to teachers, schools, school authorities, or policy makers. *Educational Psychology Review*. https://doi.org/10.1007/s10648-023-09776-8

Section A

Programs Within Particular Traditional Subjects

2

Science

Science is one of the most popular subjects for the introduction of metacognitive approaches.

Background

A review of research on science education was offered by Zohar and Barzilai (2013), but they offered a map of areas of metacognition in science rather than summarizing outcomes. They conducted a systematic analysis of 178 studies from 2000–2012, with 66 chosen for in-depth analysis, but only from the ERIC (Education Resources Information Centre, https://eric.ed.gov) database. However, only three studies included preschool students and only eight lower elementary school students. The development of metacognitive skills was one of the central aims of metacognition research, which was not the case in previous reviews that focused more on metacognitive knowledge. Biology was the discipline most frequently studied, followed by physics, chemistry and earth sciences, in that order.

A wide range of instructional practices were employed to enhance metacognitive knowledge and skill:

(a) Explicit instruction – practices to visibly and explicitly teach metacognitive knowledge or skills. Explicit

instruction need not imply "transmission" of knowledge. It can also involve many forms of constructivist practice.
(b) Practice and training – repeated training and practice, providing opportunities for activating and applying metacognitive knowledge and skills in multiple tasks, problems and contexts.
(c) Metacognitive prompts – metacognitive prompts were defined as questions, cues, or probes introduced by the teacher, by student peers, or in a computerized environment, with the aim of fostering metacognitive thinking.
(d) Teacher-led metacognitive discussions – discussions in which teachers talked with their students about their thinking and learning in order to encourage and develop metacognitive thinking.
(e) Student-led metacognitive discussions – sometimes, metacognitive discussions were led and managed by the learners themselves, usually in planned structured or semi-structured ways.
(f) Metacognitive writing – practices included writing of journals, reports or short reflections in which learners had opportunities to reflect on, describe and analyze their thinking and learning.
(g) Metacognitive modeling – metacognitive modeling refers to activities in which the teacher demonstrated how he/she activated and applied metacognitive knowledge and skills in the course of learning.
(h) Concept mapping and other visual representations – the use of concept maps, graphic organizers, flowcharts and additional visual representations in order to help learners represent and share their thinking and learning.
(i) ICT use for metacognitive instruction – digital information and communication technologies were used in teaching for facilitating metacognition.

The most prominent method was the use of metacognitive cues and prompts in the course of instruction, embedding these in science learning. These prompts were usually metacognitive cues, questions or checklists that were used by the students during activities such as problem solving, experimentation, inquiry learning, reading science texts, writing reports and reflections, or discussing science topics. Metacognition could be construed either as an input or as an output of a method. Studies using controlled research designs were still insufficient. There were too few studies among young learners in preschool and the early years of elementary school. Also, there were very few studies of teachers' knowledge and professional development regarding metacognition. Avargil et al. (2018) offered a further review, but in this case only searched three major science journals, finding 23 papers and six chapters, and again did not summarize outcomes.

Turning to individual papers, Haidar and Al Naqabi (2008) researched 162 students in four 11th grade classes: two from a boys' school (n = 80) and two from a girls' school (n = 82). The aim was to investigate their understanding of stoichiometry, their use of metacognitive strategies and the influence of their use of metacognitive strategies. Two instruments were used, the first to measure students' understanding of stoichiometry and the second to measure students' use of metacognitive strategies. The students' understanding of stoichiometry was low. They then used five metacognitive strategies: awareness of cognition, planning, monitoring and self-checking, self-appraisal, and engagement in the task. Planning and monitoring/self-checking were the most used and predicted student success in understanding of stoichiometry. There was a significant correlation between students' overall use of metacognitive strategies and students' understanding of stoichiometry.

A study of the effect of metacognitive training on 49 teachers (92% female) in training to be elementary teachers was undertaken by Abd-El-Khalicka and Akerson (2009). It assessed the effect of training in, and subsequent use of, metacognitive strategies in the development of views of nature of science. There was random assignment to intervention and comparison groups. Students in the intervention group received instruction in, and used, three metacognitive strategies. The Views of Nature of Science Questionnaire and the Metacognitive Awareness Inventory were used pre and post. Significantly more intervention group students explicated more informed views of the target aspects of the nature of science. These substantial changes were coupled with significantly increased Metacognitive Awareness Inventory scores for the intervention group participants. Of course, we do not know if these gains were sustained once these students actually became teachers.

A larger-scale study with 300 secondary school biology students and six teachers from six secondary schools was reported by Okafor and Agboghoroma (2023), based on Prior Knowledge, Exploration, Discussion, Dissatisfaction and Application. Students in the experimental group were taught using a metacognitive instructional strategy, while control group students were taught using the lecture method. The Metacognitive Biology Achievement Test was employed pre-post with intervention and control groups. The metacognitive approach was more effective than the traditional lecture format.

Specimen Program

Our specimen program is a study undertaken in India with metacognitive scaffolding by Uddin et al. (2022), who worked with ninth-grade (14–16 years old) students in chemistry. Scaffolding is the process where the teacher gives cues, prompts or hints to help the learner discover what is required for themselves, with less scaffolding being required the nearer the learner is to independent discovery. Metacognitive scaffolding is when these cues, hints or prompts relate to issues of metacognition, i.e., they are not concerned with the content of the inquiry in itself. According to research, metacognitive scaffolding has a favorable influence on students' problem-solving processes.

Such scaffolding improves metacognitive capacity, academic self-efficacy and learning achievement. It also shows that pupils with various cognitive types have similar learning outcomes. However, from the research literature, it seems a very limited number of studies have been conducted on the use of metacognitive scaffolding in teaching science at the secondary level, especially through a detective approach involving handling readily available materials in their homes and communities.

Consequently, the effectiveness of metacognitive scaffolding on learning outcomes for ninth-grade learners in the detective learning of acids, bases and salts in physical science was investigated by examining their various properties such as taste, neutralization, identification, solubility in water and indicator tests through the students' continuous involvement and monitoring the process.

A pre-test-post-test control group quasi-experimental design was applied in this study. One hundred and seven students from two government-sponsored co-educational Hindi medium schools were the sample, divided into intervention and control groups. Metacognitive scaffolding was the independent variable, and learning outcome was the dependent variable. There was only a short treatment period, i.e., ten weeks at the rate of one hour daily on working days in both schools.

Both groups were pre-tested on a test comprising 20 multiple-choice items with four options and one mark for each item, to see if their understanding of acids, bases, and salts was the same. The reliability coefficient was 0.86 and the validity 0.93 (maximum 1). Metacognitive scaffolding was used with the intervention group, while a conventional lecture method was used with the control group. In the former group, the researcher created a conducive learning environment to encourage the learners to actively participate and interact with one another. It was common in the traditional group to use a blackboard and charts as well as ask students questions in between lectures to convey information about the topic.

Following the intervention, the same set of questions was employed as a post-test for both groups. A self-developed and standardized competency-based test for assessing the learning outcomes consisted of 25 multiple-choice items with one mark for each correct response and zero mark for each wrong response, and a self-developed reaction scale. A five-point rating scale was also administered for collecting student perceptions. The effectiveness of metacognitive scaffolding in terms of learning outcomes in physical science was evaluated by comparing the mean scores of learners in the two groups. The results showed that the intervention group performed considerably better than the traditional lecture group. Not only was the difference statistically significant, the effect size was eta-squared 0.09, which would be regarded as above medium and heading towards large.

To understand the reaction of intervention group learners towards the use of metacognitive scaffolding in the teaching and learning of physical science, a five-point scale comprised of 20 statements (10 positive and 10 negative) was used. On a five-point scale, participants rated each statement on how strongly they agreed or disagreed on various aspects of metacognitive strategies (planning, monitoring, and evaluation). About 82% of students supported the idea that the equipment used during the teaching and learning process was appropriate and 73% of learners agreed with the rate of speed of the demonstration. Hindi was supported by 64% as the medium of instruction because it was more comfortable and easily understood as their home language. The maximum percentage of students stated that the voice of the demonstrator was clear, the content coverage was appropriate, stimulus variation was appropriate during the teaching-learning process, teacher support was helpful during the demonstration, examples discussed in the classroom were given from real life and blackboard work was appropriate. Probing questions asked during the teaching-learning process were very helpful for building concepts according to 73% of students. About 64% of learners said that peer group interaction during the demonstration helped in quality learning. Student involvement in carrying out the activities was supported by 91%, in that it helped in learning effectively. Most learners (64%) understood the need to consolidate the main points once again at the end of the class and the same number disagreed that the situation-based questions asked after the completion of the class were not appropriate for evaluation. Hence, most of the learners responded favorably to the use of metacognitive scaffolding.

Implementation

The roles of both teachers and students are equally important in executing metacognitive interventions in classroom instruction.

The teacher helps in identifying the learning gaps of the students, provides suitable facilities, and assists in every stage of their learning. Metacognitive interventions are multifunctional in nature, and they can be applied to ensure competency as well as quality learning. Research studies have identified various metacognitive interventions for the improvement of quality learning. Some of these strategies or interventions are briefly discussed below.

1. Thinking aloud – an instructional technique in which students express their thoughts or feelings as they work on a learning task or assignment. It is used by teachers and learners to promote metacognitive awareness.
2. Concept mapping – an innovative instructional technique applied by the teacher to present the content knowledge of the subject in pictorial forms such as graphs, maps, flowcharts, tree diagrams, Venn diagrams, etc. It helps in developing critical thinking, creativity and meta-memory toward the connectivity between concepts and sub-concepts.
3. Self-assessment – an auto-monitoring technique used by learners to observe and evaluate their own progress and shortcomings while learning.
4. Brainstorming – a teaching-learning strategy in which students in small groups discuss an issue, share their perspectives, and learn concepts in cooperative and collaborative ways.
5. Reflective writing – an effective instructional strategy where the learners freely share their experience about a particular issue, concept, or event in the form of a written document.
6. Modeling – an instructional technique through which learners are actively engaged in learning and acquire new concepts presented by the teacher.
7. Metacognitive scaffolding – an important instructional strategy, with a close link to the constructivist approach to teaching, where the students get desired assistance from the teacher in completing a task.

8. Self-questioning – an auto-learning approach where students are inspired to ask themselves questions and assess their own progress and deficiencies in learning. This strategy helps promote the learners' self-regulated learning skills.
9. Wrapper – this strategy is concerned with the auto-monitoring behavior of the learners in the classroom. It is generally used in the written examination, where examinees are inspired to think critically about the responses given in their answer scripts.
10. Explicit instruction – an instructional strategy where the teachers apply appropriate steps in the teaching-learning process, like demonstration, modeling, illustration, etc., keeping in mind the psychological development of the learners.

Metacognitive scaffolding involves providing pupils with temporary assistance until they are able to complete tasks on their own. It implies that teachers use scaffolding so that learners can eventually perform the task unaided appropriately. Scaffolding has been further subdivided into four categories: Conceptual, Metacognitive, Procedural and Strategic. Metacognitive scaffolding helps with planning, monitoring and evaluation. Procedural scaffolding places an emphasis on using available learning resources. Strategic scaffolding suggests how to deal with tasks as well as problems.

Students acquired experiential learning joyfully and efficiently using the detective learning approach by receiving assistance from the teacher. The role of the teacher during the activities was that of a facilitator and guide, and he created an attractive learning environment in the classroom to ensure quality learning in physical science. Activities were self-performed by the students of the experimental group in the classroom with necessary assistance from the teacher.

According to the findings of this study, metacognitive scaffolding was a crucial factor in enhancing students' learning, but previously students rarely used this strategy unless they were encouraged to do so. Metacognitive scaffolding, if effectively applied by teachers in the context of teaching science subjects such as physics and chemistry at the secondary level, could significantly improve student performance. Research on the remaining dimensions of metacognitive strategies (thinking aloud, concept mapping, self-assessment, brainstorming, reflective writing, modeling, metacognitive scaffolding, self-questioning, wrappers, etc.) might be conducted for solving a variety of problems in different settings.

References

Abd-El-Khalicka, F., & Akerson, V. (2009). The influence of metacognitive training on preservice elementary teachers' conceptions of nature of science. *International Journal of Science Education*, *31*(16), 2161–2184. doi: 10.1080/09500690802563324

Avargil, S., Lavi, R., & Dori, Y. J. (2018). Students' metacognition and metacognitive strategies in science education. In Y. J. Dori, Z. Mevarech, & D. Baker (Eds.), *Cognition, Metacognition, and Culture in STEM Education* (pp. 33–64). Cham, Switzerland: Springer.

Haidar, A. H., & Al Naqabi, A. K. (2008). Emirati high school students' understandings of stoichiometry and the influence of metacognition on their understanding. *Research in Science & Technological Education*, *26*(2), 215–237. doi: 10.1080/02635140802037393

Okafor, S. N., & Agboghoroma, T. E. (2023). Effect of metacognitive instructional strategy using PEEDA on biology students' achievement in Delta State. *International Journal of Social Science and Education Research Studies*, *3*(1), 25–31. https://doi.org/10.55677/ijssers/V03I1Y2023-04

Uddin, M. J., Panda, B. N., & Agarwal, P. C. (2022). Detective learning of the concepts of acids, bases and salts in physical science by ninth-grade students using a metacognitive instructional strategy: A quasi-experimental study. *Journal of Education, Society and Behavioural Science*, *35*(12), 96–107. doi: 10.9734/JESBS/2022/v35i121199

Zohar, A., & Barzilai, S. (2013). A review of research on metacognition in science education: Current and future directions. *Studies in Science Education*, *49*(2), 121–169. doi: 10.1080/03057267.2013.847261

3

Mathematics

Mathematics is the next most popular subject for including metacognition after science.

Background

There are four reviews of research on metacognition in mathematics, but some take a section of mathematics or participant age, so they are not complete reviews. The purpose of Lee et al.'s (2018) meta-analysis was to examine the impact of metacognitive training on students' algebraic reasoning. Eighteen studies with 22 effect sizes were selected for inclusion. Included studies were quite evenly spread from kindergarten through eighth grade, although first, second and fourth grades were absent. The overall effect size was 0.97, which would be considered large. Metacognitive training had a significant positive impact on student algebraic reasoning.

The meta-analytic review of Ohtani and Hisasaka (2018) *inter alia* investigated the relationship between metacognition and mathematics and found it was moderated by the choice of measurement tools. Online tools (including think-aloud) had particularly strong correlations ($r = 0.53$) with academic performance. Accuracy measures ($r = 0.43$) and interviews ($r = 0.45$) correlated moderately with academic performance, while broad-based measures showed lower correlation ($r = 0.21$). Although offline methods correlated only weakly with academic performance ($r = 0.23$), with questionnaires showing a particularly low correlation ($r = 0.19$), 61% of the studies on children aged 4–16 years used self-report measures.

By contrast, Muncer et al. (2022) meta-analyzed a wider range of mathematics performance up to January 2020 in 31 studies, but did so only with reference to adolescents (aged 11–17 years). The quantitative synthesis of 74 effect sizes from these indicated a significantly positive correlation between metacognition and mathematics performance in adolescence ($r = .37$, $p < .001$). Online (versus offline) measures of metacognition and more complex (versus simple) measures of mathematics performance were associated with larger effect sizes.

Sercenia and Prudente (2023) examined the effectiveness of metacognitive-based interventions on students' mathematics achievement. Twenty-three studies from 2015 to 2022 were included. The overall weighted effect size was 1.36, indicating metacognitive-based intervention had a large positive effect on mathematics achievement. Further moderator analysis showed significant differences by mathematics subject area, but there were no significant differences in relation to educational level and targeted learning outcomes.

Turning to selected individual studies, in a classic paper Kramarski and Mevarech (2003) compared the effects of four instructional methods on 384 eighth-grade students' mathematical reasoning (on graph interpretation and various aspects of mathematical explanations) and metacognitive knowledge. Cooperative learning was combined with metacognitive training, individualized learning combined with metacognitive training, cooperative learning without metacognitive training and individualized learning without metacognitive training. The cooperative learning plus metacognitive training group significantly outperformed the individualized learning plus metacognitive training group, which in turn significantly outperformed the other groups. Both metacognitive groups also outperformed the other groups on graph construction (transfer tasks) and metacognitive knowledge.

Subsequently, Mevarech and Amrany (2008) examined whether 61 high school students exposed to metacognitive instruction were able to implement metacognitive processes in a delayed, stressful situation (the matriculation exam) and whether students preparing themselves for this exam attained a higher level of mathematics achievement and metacognitive awareness as a result of metacognitive instruction. Half of the students were assigned to metacognitive instruction (called IMPROVE) and the others had no explicit metacognitive guidance (control group). IMPROVE students outperformed their counterparts on mathematics achievement and regulation of cognition, but not on knowledge about cognition.

Mevarech's next study (Mevarech et al., 2010) investigated the effects of IMPROVE on 194 third (n = 110) and sixth graders' (n = 84) solution of word problems, with either consistent or inconsistent language. Half the students had IMPROVE and half "traditional" instruction. Pre- and post-tests of 16 word problems were given. At both grade levels the IMPROVE students significantly outperformed the control group, but third graders benefited more than sixth graders.

Another famous name in mathematics metacognition (Veenman) appears in the next study (Van der Stel et al., 2010). The authors comment that the role that metacognitive skills play in mathematics seemed to change over the early years of secondary education, becoming more general but also increasing with age, independent of intellectual development. A standardized intelligence test was administered to 29 second-year students (13–14 years) and 30 third-year students (14–15 years) in secondary education. Participants then solved mathematical word problems with a difficulty level adapted to their age group. Think-aloud protocols were collected and analyzed on the frequency and quality of metacognitive activities. Another series of mathematical word problems served as post-test. The frequency of metacognitive activities, especially those of planning and evaluation, increased with age. Intelligence was a strong predictor of mathematics performance in 13- to 14-year-olds, but less prominent in 14- to 15-year-olds. Metacognitive skill predicted mathematics performance in both age groups, but its predictive power was stronger in 14- to 15-year-olds, even on top of intelligence.

Veenman and van Cleef (2019) reaffirmed that metacognitive skills accounted for about 40% of the variance in mathematics performance for secondary school students (aged 14–15 years). There was a significant correlation between mathematics problem solving and their systematic observation measure ($r = 0.52$), the think-aloud protocol ($r = 0.71$) and the retrospective questionnaire ($r = 0.34$).

Specific Program

Arithmetical word problem solving is a complex cognitive task that involves several cognitive processes not specific to mathematical abilities. Reading comprehension is involved, for instance, because the student must first understand the wording of the problem to construct a representation of it. But the information must also be maintained, processed and updated, and a series of control processes is involved in arithmetical problem solving. A correct solution plan must be identified and monitored. Solving word problems can be improved by focusing on metacognition, on general strategies related to the steps involved in solving a problem, or on the production of visual-schematic representations of a problem.

Cornoldi et al. (2015) examined the feasibility of improving word problem-solving skills in school children by means of a training program that addressed general and specific abilities involved in problem solving, focusing on metacognition and working memory. The sample was 135 primary school children in eight classes in the third, fourth and fifth grades (age range 8–10 years). The classes were assigned to two groups, one attending the training program in the first three months of the study and the other serving as a waiting-list control group. In the second phase of the study, the roles of the two groups were reversed. The training program led to improvements in both metacognitive and working memory tasks, with positive effects on the ability to solve problems (which were particularly strong, with eta-squared effect size = 0.30, i.e., very large). The gains seen in the first training group were also maintained at the second post-test (after three months). The greatest training benefits were observed in the weakest children.

Implementation

The training programs consisted of eight sessions. The sessions were held collectively, but children worked on their own. At the beginning of each session, pupils were given materials specifically designed for the activities, and the trainer introduced them before they completed various exercises. To reinforce the effect of the training, the first five minutes of each session were dedicated to summarizing the main topics covered at the previous sessions. There was one session a week, and each session lasted about one hour and followed a fixed schedule. After briefly summarizing the activities involved in the previous session (5 minutes), the trainer introduced the metacognitive activities (20 minutes). Then, 10 minutes were spent on working memory exercises involving variations of classical working memory tests, such as the listening span test. The last 20 minutes were devoted to talking about components of problem solving, also referring to the previous activities on working memory and metacognition, and associating them more specifically with problem solving.

The model identified five components of problem solving: A first component related to the understanding of the text, and four other components related to the ability to represent the problem and categorize it correctly, to choose the correct solution, and to plan and monitor the procedure used. The material focused particularly on strategies related to understanding the wording of the problem (e.g., enhancing the ability to distinguish relevant from irrelevant information) and to improving the visual/schematic representation of problems. These two strategies had previously proved effective in promoting word problem-solving abilities.

The content of the activities involved in each session by intervention area is summarized below, in terms of metacognitive beliefs, working memory and problem-solving components for each session:

Session 1. Recognizing the importance of attention for problem solving. Recall without a secondary task (recall of the last words). Understanding the wording of the problem: selecting relevant information.

Session 2. Recognizing the role of self-efficacy in problem solving. Recall of words with a secondary task. Understanding the wording of the problem: selecting irrelevant information.

Session 3. Recognizing the importance of working memory in problem solving. Recall of words with a secondary task. Mental representation of the problem: building up a visual representation of the problem to insert and connect new information.

Session 4. Distinguishing between different mathematics problems; identifying the characteristics of a mathematics problem. Recall of words with a secondary task. Categorizing different mathematics problems by their structure.

Session 5. Recognizing that problems can be solved using different procedures. Recall of words with a secondary task. Identifying the phases that lead to the solution.

Session 6. Using mistakes to improve problem-solving performance. Recall of words with a secondary task. Producing more than one plan for solving a given problem.

Session 7. The importance of intrinsic motivation. Recall of words with a secondary task. Solving problems: the importance of choosing the right operations and performing them in the right order.

Session 8. The importance of recognizing factors that negatively affect school attainment, particularly in mathematics (e.g., anxiety). Recall of digits with a secondary task. The importance of monitoring problem-solving activities.

The following is an example of the specific activities involved in one of the sessions (#3) of the training program:

Metacognition. Recognizing the importance of working memory in problem solving. Children listened to a short story describing an investigation conducted by a police inspector. While listening to the story, children looked at a picture showing the characters in the story with their physical features. After hearing the story, the children were asked to remember the relevant information provided by one of the witnesses to the crime. Then, they were guided to reflect on how working memory was involved in this activity and transfer this reflection to the context of a mathematics problem, where solvers should be able to identify and recall relevant information.

Working memory. Recall of words with a secondary task. Children listened to a series of sentences. For each sentence, they had to say whether it was true or false, then recall the last word in each sentence in the correct order of presentation. The difficulty of the task, in terms of the number of words to recall, increased from two to five.

Problem-solving components. Mental representation of the problem: building up a visual representation of the problem to be able to insert and connect new information. Children were presented with a problem. After reading the text of the problem, they were given two visual representations of the same problem. The trainer promoted a comparison between the features of the two visual representations. Finally, participants tried to draw different visual representations of a second problem.

References

Cornoldi, C., Carretti, B., Drusi, S., & Tencati, C. (2015). Improving problem solving in primary school students: The effect of a training programme focusing on metacognition and working memory. *British Journal of Educational Psychology*, *85*, 424–439. doi: 10.1111/bjep.12083

Kramarski, B., & Mevarech, Z. R. (2003). Enhancing mathematical reasoning in the classroom: The effects of cooperative learning and metacognitive training. *American Education Research Journal*, *40*, 281–310. doi: 10.3102/00028312040001281

Lee, Y. J., Capraro, M. M., Capraro, R. M., & Bicer, A. (2018). A meta-analysis: Improvement of students' algebraic reasoning through metacognitive training. *International Education Studies*, *11*(10), 42–49. https://doi.org/10.5539/ies.v11n10p42

Mevarech, Z. R., & Amrany, C. (2008). Immediate and delayed effects of meta-cognitive instruction on regulation of cognition and mathematics achievement. *Metacognition and Learning*, *3*, 147–157. doi: 10.1007/s11409-008-9023-3

Mevarech, Z. R., Terkieltaub, S., Vinberger, T., & Nevet, V. (2010). The effects of meta-cognitive instruction on third and sixth graders solving word problems. *ZDM Mathematics Education*, *42*, 195–203. doi: 10.1007/s11858-010-0244-y

Muncer, G., Higham, P. A., Gosling, C. J., Cortese, S., Wood-Downie, H., & Hadwin, J. A. (2022). A meta-analysis investigating the association between metacognition and math performance in adolescence. *Educational Psychology Review*, *34*, 301–334. https://doi.org/10.1007/s10648-021-09620-x

Ohtani, K., & Hisasaka, T. (2018). Beyond intelligence: A meta-analytic review of the relationship among metacognition, intelligence, and academic performance. *Metacognition and Learning*, *13*, 179–212. https://doi.org/10.1007/s1140 9-018-9183-8

Sercenia, J. C., & Prudente, M. S. (2023). Effectiveness of the metacognitive-based pedagogical intervention on mathematics achievement: A meta-analysis. *International Journal of Instruction*, *16*(4), 561–578.

Van der Stel, M., Veenman, M. V. J., Deelen, K., & Haenen, J. (2010). The increasing role of metacognitive skills in math: A cross-sectional study from a developmental perspective. *ZDM Mathematics Education*, *42*, 219–229. doi: 10.1007/s11858-009-0224-2

Veenman, M. V. J., & van Cleef, D. (2019). Measuring metacognitive skills for mathematics: Students' self-reports vs. online assessment methods. *ZDM Mathematics Education*, *51*(4), 691–701. https://doi.org/10.1007/s11858-018-1006-5

4
Language, Reading and Writing

In this chapter we review the evidence on Language, Reading and Writing, in that order.

Background

Language
Raoofi et al. (2014) reviewed 33 studies from 1999–2013. However, most were in higher education, with only two in elementary school and eight in high school. At this time, questionnaires were the most widely used tool. All of the studies reported that metacognitive instruction or treatment significantly improved language performance. However, none of these studies were truly experimental, that is, participants were not randomly assigned to treatment and control groups and other variables were not controlled. Small sample size and lack of follow-up were issues.

More recent individual papers have tended to be of better quality. Singh et al. (2020) investigated the effects of metacognitive strategies and gender differences on ESL students' listening comprehension. The study employed a quasi-experimental design consisting of pre-test and post-test control, experimental groups and focus group interviews. Sixty-two form 6 randomly selected students participated. Students exposed to metacognitive strategies showed a statistically significant difference from controls. There was no difference by gender. Findings from student interviews showed three metacognitive factors applied: person knowledge, task knowledge and strategic knowledge.

The role of metacognitive monitoring in language abilities in 5- to 7-year-old native and non-native speakers was investigated by Buehler et al. (2023). Data came from the German National Educational Panel Study (n = 9167; 49.6% male). Earlier language abilities predicted later metacognitive monitoring for native but not for non-native speakers. Conversely, metacognitive monitoring predicted language abilities for non-native but not for native speakers. Different mechanisms appeared to be driving native and non-native speakers' metacognitive monitoring development.

Reading

A meta-analysis of 17 studies of metacognitive strategy instruction in reading comprehension in a computerized environment was offered by Lan et al. (2014). In a world in which electronic reading is becoming increasingly common, the reading platform has shifted from traditional text to hypertext. However, it is important to know if reading strategies required by e-text are different from those required by a hard copy book. The majority of the participants were undergraduate students, but participants from secondary schools numbered 412 (34%) and 184 (15%) were from elementary schools. Instruction was implemented only once in more than half of the studies (n = 10). Two studies implemented instruction more frequently but did not report how often. The remaining five studies reported instruction frequencies ranging from two to four times per week and the average duration was 9.5 weeks.

The metacognitive strategies implemented by the 17 studies could be categorized into three main groups: (1) self-regulation, (2) strategy cues with think-aloud, and (3) vocabulary and comprehension support. Self-regulation had 12 effect sizes which averaged 0.67. Think-aloud had only two effect sizes which averaged 2.24, so this result is unreliable. Vocabulary and comprehension support had 11 very various effect sizes which averaged 0.56. Comparing computerized with hard copy text, there was no difference in outcome. Some of these studies had significant drawbacks.

Turning to individual studies, Keskin (2013) studied 371 fifth- to eighth-grade students, investigating the use of metacognitive strategies in reading, academic and general reading attitudes, and school success. Results showed that the use of metacognitive strategies in reading was influential on both academic and general reading attitudes. Reading attitudes were influential on school success, and appeared to mediate the relationship between metacognitive strategies and school success. However, the knowledge and use of metacognitive strategies in reading contributed to positive reading attitudes, and these positive attitudes led students to read in higher volume and diversity, so school success was affected positively.

Carretti et al. (2014) studied the feasibility of improving text comprehension in school children by comparing the efficacy of two training programs, both involving metacognition and working memory, but one based on listening comprehension, the other on reading comprehension. The study involved 159 pupils attending eight classes in the fourth and fifth grades (age range 9–11 years). The listening and reading programs focused on the same abilities/processes, particularly metacognitive knowledge and control and working memory. Training programs were implemented by school teachers, under the supervision of experts. A control group completed standard text comprehension activities. Both training programs were effective in improving the children's achievement, but training in reading comprehension generated greater gains than the listening comprehension program.

A small-scale study of 25 grade 5 EFL students was conducted by Teng (2020), examining the effects of metacognitive reading strategy instruction on English language learners' reading comprehension in a Hong Kong international school. Metacognitive instruction was incorporated into ten reading lessons. Data came from notes learners took during reading, post-reading reflection reports, teacher-facilitated group discussions and two types of reading tests. These young learners articulated several knowledge factors that influenced their reading and reported a better understanding of the nature and demands of reading, a deeper awareness of metacognitive knowledge in improving reading and increased confidence in handling reading. The learners also showed enhanced reading performance compared to those in a control group without metacognitive intervention.

Writing

Many studies of the Self-Regulated Strategy Development (SRSD) model for developing metacognitive approaches to writing are reported in Graham and Harris (2003). For teachers, SRSD has six Stages of Instruction: Develop and Activate Knowledge, Discuss It, Model It, Memorize It, Support It and Independent Performance. The average effect size for writing quality at post-test across the 15 studies was 1.20. Thus, SRSD had a strong impact on improving the writing quality of students. There was no difference between impact for learning disabled and for regular writers, nor between younger and older writers. Improvements tended to be maintained for the majority of students over time, with some students needing booster sessions for longer-term maintenance. Students also showed generalization across settings, people and writing media.

However, there were no general review papers in writing. A chapter by van Kraayenoord et al. (2011) focused on 18 students aged 9 years 9 months to 13 years 9 months with learning difficulties (15 males and three females). Findings indicated that students' writing skills improved in two areas following the implementation of the teacher's metacognitive instruction. They improved both in the use of contextual conventions and in their use of contextual language. The improvements in writing performance were found in both the spontaneous stories produced by the students under standardized test conditions and in samples of their classroom writing, although, interestingly, the students' improvement was more pronounced in the latter. However, metacognitive knowledge about writing showed no improvement.

A study by Bui and Kong (2019) employed a 12-week intervention involving metacognitive training in peer review interaction in second language writing with 18 first year secondary students (aged 12–13 years). Training focused on metacognitive knowledge and self-regulation. The metacognitive training in peer review interaction increased students' level of engagement and collaboration during five peer review tasks. It also encouraged students to provide more content-related feedback than language-related feedback. Finally, the students were able to seriously consider peer feedback when revising the peer-reviewed drafts, but written feedback had a much higher chance of being incorporated than did oral feedback.

Two research questions were addressed by Colognesia et al. (2020): (1) What effects do metacognitive questions have on students' writing skills? and (2) How do students respond to metacognitive questions? An experiment was conducted with 43 11- to 12-year-old students (in two classes in the same school) writing in a particular genre: book reviews. For three weeks they experienced instruction combining identified principles of effective writing instruction. They then rewrote their text several times, but in one group metacognitive questions were introduced before, during, and after writing, unlike in the other class. A total of 172 written productions were analyzed. Results showed that students in both conditions made significant progress. However, in the metacognitive condition, students made more progress.

Specific Program

The effectiveness of self-regulated learning interventions led by teachers and applicable to three subjects (writing, mathematics, reading) was investigated by Lee et al. (2023).

The authors argued that self-regulated learning should be taught with specific subject matters or content domains because students developed cognitive skills, behavioral tactics and motivational beliefs in a highly domain- and context-specific manner. Additionally, teacher-led self-regulated learning interventions exhibited weaker effect sizes than research-led interventions. Students who have learned about self-regulated learning as decontextualized general strategies might struggle to transfer and apply the knowledge to specific subject domains. Upper elementary school students (n = 214) participated in a series of three intervention studies (n1 = 70, n2 = 69, n3 = 75).

Trained teachers implemented the interventions – incorporating explicit instructions about domain-specific strategies in persuasive writing (Study 1), solving mathematical word problems (Study 2) and reading comprehension (Study 3). Participants were assigned to one of the three groups: regular classroom instruction, domain-specific strategy instruction and strategy instruction incorporating self-regulated learning instruction. The latter group used more self-regulated strategies, performed better in achievement tests and were less distracted by task-irrelevant thoughts than the other groups. This study was interesting in that it focused on three separate subjects, incorporated not only metacognitive knowledge training but also self-regulation training, and used regular classroom teachers as deliverers of the intervention.

Implementation

Implementation was based on the Eight-Phase Cyclical Model of Self-Regulated Learning, attributed to Zimmerman (2013). Initially, the Forethought phase includes Self-Assessment, Task Analysis, Goal Setting and Strategic Planning. Then the Performance Control phase includes Strategy Implementation and Strategy Monitoring, with a feedback loop of Strategy Adjustment. Then the Self-Reflection phase incorporates Outcome Evaluation.

In the following, STR Group = Strategy, and STR + SRL Group = Strategy + Self-Regulated Learning.

Writing
Sessions 1–3
STR: Regular class instruction.

STR + SRL: Introduction to SRL: Teacher instruction about SRL – What is SRL and why is it important? What are the eight phases of SRL? How can we use the eight-phase SRL for writing an essay? How do the eight phases circulate and interact with each other?

Sessions 4–5
STR and STR + SRL: Practice strategies: Teacher instruction about three writing strategies and practice strategies with a short writing exercise. Brainstorming. Drawing a mind map. Having a conversation about the topic with friends.

Sessions 6–7
STR and STR + SRL: How to write a persuasive essay: Teacher instruction about writing a persuasive essay – What is a persuasive essay and why is it necessary? What are the main features of a persuasive essay? What is the format and composition of a persuasive essay?

Sessions 8–12
STR: Writing practice: Write a persuasive essay every day using the three writing strategies.

STR and STR + SRL: Writing practice: Write a persuasive essay every day using the three writing strategies and eight phases of SRL as a whole process. Teacher feedback about student SRL.

Mathematics

Session 1
STR: Overall introduction to the program and teacher instruction about the "drawing a diagram" strategy.

STR + SRL: Overall introduction to the program and teacher instruction about the "drawing a diagram" strategy. Introduction to SRL: Teacher instruction about SRL – What is SRL and why is it important? What are the eight phases of SRL? How can we use the eight-phase SRL for solving mathematical word problems?

Session 2
STR: Practice: Solve word problems using the "drawing a diagram" strategy.

STR + SRL: Practice: Solve word problems using the "drawing a diagram" strategy. Getting used to the eight-phase SRL: Memorize and get used to the eight phases of SRL while solving the word problems.

Session 3
STR: Instruction: Teacher instruction about the "making a table" strategy.

STR + SRL: Instruction: Teacher instruction about the "making a table" strategy. Introduction to the cyclical model of SRL: Teacher instruction about how the eight phases circulate and interact with each other.

Session 4
STR: Practice: Solve word problems using the "making a table" strategy.

STR + SRL: Practice: Solve word problems using the "making a table" strategy. Practice cyclical SRL while solving the word problems. Teacher feedback about student SRL.

Session 5
STR: Instruction & practice: Teacher instruction about the "finding a rule" strategy and student practice.

STR + SRL: Instruction & practice: Teacher instruction about the "finding a rule" strategy and student practice. Practice SRL cycle II: Practice cyclical SRL while solving the word problems. Teacher feedback about student SRL.

Session 6
STR: Solve word problems using the three strategies.

STR + SRL: Solve word problems using the three strategies and SRL as a whole process. Teacher feedback about student SRL.

Reading
TWA was the **T**hink Before, **W**hile, and **A**fter reading strategy.

Session 1
STR and STR + SRL: Introduction to the TWA strategy: Teacher instruction about the TWA strategy.

Session 2
STR: Read a news article using TWA. Introduction to SRL.

STR + SRL: Teacher instruction about SRL – What is SRL and why is it important? What are the eight phases of SRL? How can we use the eight-phase SRL for reading a text?

Session 3
STR: Read a discussion paper using the TWA strategy.

STR + SRL: Read a news article using the TWA strategy. Getting used to the eight-phase SRL: Memorize and get used to the eight phases of SRL while reading a news article.

Session 4
STR: Read a story text using the TWA strategy.

STR + SRL: Read a discussion paper using the TWA strategy. Introduction to the cyclical model of SRL: Teacher instruction about how the eight phases circulate and interact with each other.

Session 5
STR: Read a story text using the TWA strategy.

STR + SRL: Read a story text using the TWA strategy. Practice SRL cycle I: Practice cyclical SRL while reading a story.

Session 6
STR: Read an essay using the TWA strategy.

STR + SRL: Read a story text using the TWA strategy. Practice SRL cycle II: Practice how to diagnose one's phase accurately and generalize SRL.

Session 7
STR: Read an expository text using the TWA strategy.

STR + SRL: Read an essay using the TWA strategy. Practice SRL as a whole process while reading an essay using the TWA strategy.

Session 8
STR: Regular class instruction.

STR + SRL: Read an expository text using TWA. Practice SRL as a whole process while reading an expository text using the TWA strategy.

References

Buehler, F. J., Orth, U., Krauss, S., & Roebers, C. M. (2023). The longitudinal relation between language abilities and metacognitive monitoring in native and non-native speaking children. *OSF Preprints*. www.osf.io

Bui, G., & Kong, A. (2019). Metacognitive instruction for peer review interaction in L2 writing. *Journal of Writing Research*, *11*(2), 357–392. doi: 10.17239/jowr-2019.11.02.05

Carretti, B., Caldarola, N., Tencati, C., & Cornoldi, C. (2014). Improving reading comprehension in reading and listening settings: The effect of two training programmes focusing on metacognition and working memory. *British Journal of Educational Psychology*, *84*, 194–210. doi: 10.1111/bjep.12022

Colognesia, S., Piret, C., Demorsy, S., & Barbier, E. (2020). Teaching writing – with or without metacognition? An exploratory study of 11- to 12-year-old students writing a book review. *International Electronic Journal of Elementary Education*, *12*(5), 459–470. doi: 10.26822/iejee.2020562136

Graham, S., & Harris, K. R. (2003). Students with learning disabilities and the process of writing: A meta-analysis of SRSD studies. In H. L. Swanson, K. R. Harris, & S. Graham (Eds.), *Handbook of Learning Disabilities* (pp. 323–344). New York: Guilford.

Keskin, H. K. (2013). Impacts of reading metacognitive strategies and reading attitudes on school success. *International Journal of Academic Research Part B*, *5*(5), 312–317. doi: 10.7813/2075-4124.2013/5-5/B.48

Lan, Y. C., Lo, Y. L., & Hsu, Y. S. (2014). The effects of meta-cognitive instruction on students' reading comprehension in computerized reading contexts: A quantitative meta-analysis. *Educational Technology & Society*, *17*(4), 186–202. https://www.jstor.org/stable/jeductechsoci.17.4.186

Lee, M. H., Lee, S. Y., Kim, J. E., & Lee, H. J. (2023). Domain-specific self-regulated learning interventions for elementary school students. *Learning and Instruction*, *88*, 101810. https://doi.org/10.1016/j.learninstruc.2023.101810

Raoofi, S., Chan, S. H., Mukundan, J., & Rashid, S. M. (2014). Metacognition and second/foreign language learning. *English Language Teaching*, *7*(1), 36–49. http://dx.doi.org/10.5539/elt.v7n1p36

Singh, C. K. S., Ong, E. T., Mulyadi, D., Kiong, T. T., Wong, W. L., Singh, T. S. M., & Chen, M. J. (2020). Effects of metacognitive strategies and gender differences on English as a Second Language (ESL) students' listening comprehension. *Pertanika Journal of Social Sciences & Humanities*, *30*(S1), 81–97. www.pertanika.upm.edu.my

Teng, M. F. (2020). The benefits of metacognitive reading strategy awareness instruction for young learners of English as a second language. *Literacy*, *54*(1), 29–39. https://doi.org/10.1111/lit.12181

van Kraayenoord, C. E., Moni, K. B., Jobling, A., Elkins, J., Koppenhaver, D., & Miller, R. (2011). The writing achievement, metacognitive knowledge of writing and motivation of middle-school students with learning difficulties. In C. Wyatt-Smith, J. Elkins, & S. Gunn (Eds.), *Multiple Perspectives on Difficulties in Learning Literacy and Numeracy* (pp. 213–234). Dordrecht: Springer.

Zimmerman, B. J. (2013). From cognitive modeling to self-regulation: A social cognitive career path. *Educational Psychologist*, *48*(3), 135–147. https://doi.org/10.1080/00461520.2013.794676

Section B

Methods Across the Traditional Curriculum

5
Dialog and Think-Aloud

We referred to Discourse, Dialog and Argumentation as a common thread in many interventions in the Discussion chapter (ch. 15) of the book on cognition preceding this one: *Improving Thinking in the Classroom: What Works for Enhancing Cognition*. We raise it again here, and add to it the notion of Think-Aloud – verbalizing thoughts as students wrestle with the problems of thinking a challenge throws up.

Dialog is typically between two or more people, but more subtle forms also exist. When someone talks to themselves as they try to solve a problem, arguably that articulation of their thought process constitutes an internal dialog. As Vygotsky noted, you only really know something when you are able to say it. Thus, this kind of internal self-talk can be helpful.

Definitions

A dialog is any conversation between two or more people, often intended to resolve a problem by negotiation. Each person's ideas are tested against the understanding of the other person(s), and hopefully weak or false ideas are eliminated while strong ideas are agreed between the pair or group. Dialog can be between teacher and student or between student and student (and, these days, between a student and various forms of artificial intelligence).

DOI: 10.4324/9781003402190-7

Think-aloud – if you think aloud, you deliberately express your thoughts immediately as they occur to you, rather than thinking first and then speaking. You narrate your thought processes in their entirety as they are happening. You might do this while you are actually in the process of trying to solve a problem. This gives an insight into how your mind is working, how you are going about problem solving, what lines of thought lead to positive outcomes and what lines of thought are not successful. Of course, pairs and groups can do think-alouds together.

Background

Dialog

Calil and Myhill (2020) undertook a study on textual genetics, the terminology for which included: textual object, erasure (insertion or deletion), school manuscript (draft writing), enunciation (interactive statement) and linearization (linear movement in either direction). The erasures were then classified. The study sought to understand what newly-literate writers' textual modifications (erasures) and oral comments revealed about their metalinguistic understanding of writing. Six classroom sequences of narrative writing composition were recorded, using both video and audio, capturing both the unfolding texts and the dyadic dialog about these texts in the collaborative writing context. Although the young writers' metalinguistic thinking was dominated by graphic-spatial concerns, there was also evidence of emerging broader metalinguistic thinking across a range of categories.

A tool to visually display the characteristics of peer verbal interactions was developed by Celepkolu et al. (2021). Young learners often face challenges with taking turns in conversation, openly listening to ideas and respecting different viewpoints. Obtaining feedback about these issues might help interactive dialog. A new interactive visualization application was presented that supported children in reflecting on their collaborative dialog from a recent prior interaction. The tool analyzed children's completed dialog and then presented temporal information about their interaction with their partner. Two studies with

36 seventh-grade children were implemented. The participants collaboratively completed computing activities. Think-aloud sessions to investigate children's perceptions, preferences and expectations of the collaborative dialog visualizations were conducted. Dialog visualizations appeared to hold promise for helping children increase their awareness of collaborative dialog and set their own goals regarding ways they would like to improve.

McIntyre et al. (2021) compared two studies with 65 teachers from six secondary schools in the Netherlands, taking two different approaches to video-stimulated think-aloud. Participating teachers in one study thought out loud whilst watching others' videos of actual classroom teaching a second time and being recorded. Participating teachers in the other study thought out loud whilst watching their own gaze patterns overlaid onto own-perspective video recordings of their own teaching, which were captured by mobile eye-tracking technology shortly before their think-aloud session. Five overarching categories were explored: the depth with which teachers process classroom information; themes and focus (for example regarding students' attention and discipline and the teacher's role); timescale (whether past, present or future tense was used); global processing (number of viewpoints represented and the integration of different actors' perspectives); and classroom relationships (the affect observed in the classroom scenario and interactions among students and the teacher). Others' videos elicited more think-aloud responses than gaze-cued own-perspective videos, especially regarding the operational aspects of classroom teaching. Interaction analysis revealed expert–novice differences vanished when only think-aloud responses to gaze-cued own-perspective videos were considered.

Think-Aloud

In an early study, Baumann et al. (1992) investigated the effectiveness of explicit instruction in think-aloud as a means to promote elementary students' comprehension monitoring abilities. Sixty-six fourth-grade students were randomly assigned to one of three experimental groups: (a) a Think-Aloud (TA) group, in which students were taught various comprehension monitoring strategies for reading stories (e.g., self-questioning, prediction, retelling, rereading) through the medium of thinking aloud; (b) a Directed Reading-Thinking Activity (DRTA) group, in which students were taught a predict-verify strategy for reading and responding to stories; or (c) a Directed Reading Activity (DRA) group, an instructed control, in which students engaged in non-interactive, guided reading of stories. Results of effect of instruction contrasts revealed that TA and DRTA students were more skillful at comprehension monitoring than DRA students for all three measures. Although TA students had greater awareness of comprehension monitoring abilities, DRTA students' performance was equal.

Twenty-seven English learners with a reading proficiency level of Early Intermediate or higher were studied by McKeown and Gentilucci (2007). There were pre- and post-tests of the three groups of English learners. After pre-test, the students were taught to use the think-aloud strategy. Explicit teacher modeling occurred over a period of two weeks during the 50- minute reading class and lasted 20–30 minutes three days each week. Fiction and non-fiction texts were used. After every two or three lines of text, the teacher stopped and restated what she thought was happening, asked herself a question, clarified, or made a prediction, thus modeling her own meaning-making strategies for the students. During the third and fourth weeks, students began applying the think-aloud strategy to their daily reading assignments. The model stressed that good readers ask questions, determine if the information they receive constitutes new or prior knowledge, predict, clarify, and reread or retell stories. The procedure was more effective with the more advanced students.

The study of Rosenzweig et al. (2011) of students with and without learning disabilities (LD) during mathematical problem solving investigated the metacognitive abilities of students with LD as they engaged in mathematical problem solving, to determine processing differences between these students and their low- and average-achieving peers (n = 73). Students thought out loud as they solved three mathematical problems of increasing difficulty. Protocols were coded and analyzed to determine frequency of cognitive verbalizations and productive and nonproductive metacognitive verbalizations. Students with learning disability produced significantly more metacognitive verbalizations than average-achieving students. Students produced significantly more metacognitive verbalizations on the hardest three-step problem compared with the one-step problem and the two-step problem. Overall, students produced significantly more productive than nonproductive metacognitive verbalizations.

Specimen Program

Kelley et al. (2015) used think-aloud to investigate the response of elementary students to challenges in design. Previous studies had made little attempt to capture students' design thinking or dialogs as they approached and engaged in the engineering design process, so this study used concurrent think-aloud protocols. Data from seven such protocols among triads of elementary students across seven classrooms were analyzed to identify how students conceptualize design.

To assess students' transfer of learning from classroom science- and engineering-based experiences to the current challenges, the researchers employed a transfer problem and think-aloud protocol analysis. Results indicated that elementary student triad design teams were able to define a design problem, identify constraints and criteria, and generate multiple design ideas to solve the problem. Protocol timelines were examined using NVivo software to capture the sequence of the triads' coded cognitive strategies, crucial in discriminating which triads used a systematic approach from those that randomly brainstormed ideas. If engineering design is to have strong theoretical pedagogical roots, attention must be given to how students learn design and function within design, and concurrent think-aloud protocol is a promising means of assessment of such efforts.

Implementation

The sequence of instructional activities and the associated learning objectives (in terms of what students subsequently would be able to do) are given below. Each objective took one to two days.

1. Introduction to weight, mass, volume and density: Describe, measure and determine the weight, mass, volume and density of different objects; compare and contrast weight and mass.
2. Reinforcing what students know about weight, mass, volume and density: Describe and explain the density of different objects by comparing physical features and measurements, e.g., of a soccer ball, plastic golf ball, standard golf ball and bowling ball.
3. Skeletal and muscular systems and movable joints: Identify major bones and muscles in the human body; identify and locate examples of movable joints in the human body; describe how movable joints function.
4. Applying concepts of weight and mass to movable joints: Describe how kicking different sports balls influences the distance each ball travels; explain how density determines how far each ball travels.
5. Example of a prosthetic limb: Describe how a prosthetic limb operates; apply and explain the features of a movable joint to a prosthetic limb.
6. Introduction to prosthetic limb design challenge: Identify essential features of the problem (i.e., problem, client, end user, constraints, criteria) and develop an individual plan of a prototype.
7. Team planning and construction: Develop a team plan and construct a prototype.
8. Construction, testing and evaluation: Complete construction of prototype; testing prototype by kicking a plastic and standard golf ball; record and evaluate results; compare results to others in the class.
9. Communicating results: Communicate findings and gather feedback from other design teams.
10. Re-design: Develop a plan for re-design; re-design and test new prototype; compare results across class.

Task 1: Design a prosthetic leg to kick a soccer ball

A company needs assistance in designing a leg for a young child. The prosthetic leg will need to be designed so that it will be able to kick a soccer ball. Engineers have designed glasses for people who need help seeing, hearing aids for people who need help hearing, crutches and canes for people who need help with bearing weight, and artificial limbs for people who have lost a limb. Designing aids for all of these human needs requires understanding what function you are augmenting and lots of creativity. We are going to learn about the musculoskeletal system and then you will be given an opportunity to test your design skills by building a prosthetic leg and testing it by using it to kick a ball.

During the lesson you will:

- Design a prosthetic leg to kick a ball.
- Measure the volume of different types of balls.
- Find the weight of the balls.
- Kick different types of balls with your prototype to see which one goes the farthest.

Design constraints:

- The leg should hinge like a real joint (move back and forth).
- The leg is being designed to strike a ball (move the ball or propel it on its own). Typically, rubber bands would be used to make the spring-loaded leg snap to propel the ball.
- A list of items and potential monetary value is provided. Students may be asked to determine how much their design costs, and they can "buy" additional items, if needed.
- Elapsed time can be recorded for further exercises.
- The lesson is meant to design something that functions like a leg when it kicks a soccer ball.
- Students do not have to mimic anatomy.

Task 2: Paper football kicker

Your younger brother is the Paper Football Champion of his grade, but he's upset he can't play since he broke his right "kicking" finger playing basketball. His friends say if he can come up with something that flicks the football for him, they'll let him keep playing. But he knows he can't kick paper footballs with his opposite hand with any level of accuracy. He heard you talking about prosthetic limbs, so he thinks you can help him out by designing a device that will kick the paper football for him.

The Paper Football game is played using two goalposts – one 3 feet away, and one 5 feet away – so your device must be accurate to these varying lengths. Your brother is looking for the following design features for this paper football kicker.

Your design should be able to:

- Hinge like a real jointed finger that is flicking the paper football.
- Strike a paper football and propel it far enough to go through the goalposts.
- Be accurate at various distances (3–5 feet).
- Take up floor space no larger than a typical textbook.

Your task is to describe how you would design a paper football flicker to flick paper footballs different distances.

Please describe aloud how you would start the design task – where would you begin? How would you design the device to include all the features listed above? What types of tests would you conduct to ensure that your device works for both desired distances?

The think-alouds were coded according to the following nine codes:

1. Analyzing: The process of identifying, isolating, taking apart, breaking down or similar for the purpose of setting forth or clarifying the basic components of a phenomenon, problem, opportunity, object, system or point of view.
2. Computing: The process of selecting and applying mathematical symbols, operations and processes to describe, estimate, calculate, quantify, relate or evaluate in a real or abstract numerical sense.

3. Defining problem: The process of stating or defining a problem to enhance investigation leading to optimal solutions; transforming one state of affairs to another desired state.
4. Designing: The process of conceiving, creating, inventing, contriving, sketching or planning by which some practical end is attained; proposing a goal to meet societal needs, desires, problems or opportunities to do things better; a cyclic or iterative process of continuous refinement or improvement.
5. Interpreting data: The process of clarifying, explaining, evaluating or translating to provide or communicate the meaning of particular data.
6. Modeling: The process of producing or reducing an act or condition to a generalized construct which may be presented graphically in the form of a sketch, diagram or equation; or presented physically in the form of a scale model or prototype; or described in the form of a written generalization.
7. Predicting: The process of prophesying or foretelling something in advance; anticipating the future on the basis of special knowledge.
8. Questions/hypotheses: Questioning is the process of asking, interrogating, challenging or seeking answers in relation to a phenomenon, problem, opportunity, element, object, event, system or point of view.
9. Testing: The process of determining the workability of a model, system, component, product or point of view in a real or simulated environment to obtain information for clarifying or modifying design specifications.

References

Baumann, J. F., Seifert-Kessell, N., & Jones, L. A. (1992). Effect of think-aloud instruction on elementary students' comprehension monitoring abilities. *Journal of Reading Behavior*, *24*(2), 143–172. https://doi.org/10.1080/10862969209547770

Calil, E., & Myhill, D. (2020). Dialogue, erasure and spontaneous comments during textual composition: What students' metalinguistic talk reveals about newly-literate writers' understanding of revision. *Linguistics and Education*, *60*, 100875. https://doi.org/10.1016/j.linged.2020.100875

Celepkolu, M., Wiggins, J. B., Galdo, A. C., & Boyer, K. E. (2021). Designing a visualization tool for children to reflect on their collaborative dialogue. *International Journal of Child-Computer Interaction*, *27*, 100232, https://doi.org/10.1016/j.ijcci.2020.100232

Kelley, T. R., Capobianco, B. M., & Kaluf, K. J. (2015). Concurrent think-aloud protocols to assess elementary design students. *International Journal of Technology and Design Education*, *25*, 521–540. doi: 10.1007/s10798-014-9291-y

McIntyre, N. A., Draycott, B., & Wolff, C. E. (2021). Keeping track of expert teachers: Comparing the affordances of think-aloud elicited by two different video perspectives. *Learning and Instruction*, *80*, 101563. https://doi.org/10.1016/j.learninstruc.2021.101563

McKeown, R. G., & Gentilucci, J. L. (2007). Think-aloud strategy: Metacognitive development and monitoring comprehension in the middle school second-language classroom. *Journal of Adolescent & Adult Literacy*, *51*(2), 136–147. doi: 10.1598/JAAL.51.2.5

Rosenzweig, C., Krawec, J., & Montague, M. (2011). Metacognitive strategy use of eighth-grade students with and without learning disabilities during mathematical problem solving: A think-aloud analysis. *Journal of Learning Disabilities*, *44*(6), 508–520. doi: 10.1177/0022219410378445

6

Questioning

Questioning has been widely promoted as a means of developing wisdom for millennia. Unfortunately, in many school classes, often teachers ask simple questions of their students which tend to have a yes or no or otherwise short answer and elaborated responses are not encouraged. Often the teacher already has the "right" answer in mind and departures from that are not welcome. There is relatively little emphasis on having the students generate their own questions and answer them, which is doubly unfortunate as developing good questions requires as much thinking as answering them. Of course, teachers justify much of this in terms of the pressure of time and the need to get on with covering the curriculum. However, covering the curriculum is of little use if the students do not understand it – and if they do not understand it, they are unlikely to remember it. Of course, questioning can lead to more refined questioning, either by the teacher or by a peer.

Definition

Questioning is the act of inquiring, asking, interrogating or examining – the investigation of a problem. Socratic questioning is a heuristic method that focuses on discovering answers by asking questions. It is named after Socrates (470–399 BC), who believed that the disciplined practice of thoughtful questioning enabled the student to examine ideas and be able to determine the validity of those ideas. Socratic questioning is a form of disciplined questioning – the teacher assumes an ignorant mindset in order to compel the student to think. Thus, a student develops the ability to acknowledge contradictions, recreate inaccurate or unfinished ideas and critically determine necessary thought. Similarly, Confucius (551–479 BC) commented that the superior person accumulated knowledge through learning and validated it through asking questions. Indeed, the Chinese expression for learning or knowledge is made up of two characters, meaning to learn and to ask questions (学问).

Background

Rosenshine et al. (1996) offered a review of 26 intervention studies in which students had been taught to generate questions as a means of improving their comprehension (although in a limited number of databases). Overall, teaching students the cognitive strategy of generating questions about the material they had read resulted in gains in comprehension, as measured by tests given at the end of the intervention. All tests were based on new material. The overall median effect size was 0.36 (with certain studies excluded) when standardized tests were used, and 0.86 when experimenter-developed comprehension tests were used.

There was no relationship between length of training and significance of results. Size of class also made no difference. The authors identified nine major instructional elements that appeared in these studies: (1) Provide procedural prompts specific to the strategy being taught, (2) Provide models of appropriate responses, (3) Anticipate potential difficulties, (4) Regulate the difficulty of the material, (5) Provide a cue card, (6) Guide student practice, (7) Provide feedback and corrections, (8) Provide and teach a checklist, and (9) Assess student mastery.

Even before this, Graesser and Person (1994) had noted that while student question-asking was infrequent in classroom environments, there was little research on questioning processes during tutoring. They collected data on 22 tutoring sessions at a middle school. There were 13 seventh-grade students who were having trouble with particular topics in their algebra class and the tutors were ten high school students. On average, a tutor had nine hours of prior tutoring experience before this project. The study investigated the questions asked in tutoring sessions on algebra. Student questions were approximately 240 times as frequent in tutoring settings as in classroom settings, whereas tutor questions were only slightly more frequent than teacher questions. Questions were classified by (a) degree of specification, (b) content, and (c) question-generation mechanism, to analyze their quality. Student achievement was positively correlated with the quality of student questions. Students partially self-regulated their learning by identifying knowledge deficits and asking questions to repair them, but they need training to improve these skills.

Shortly after this, King (1998) developed her "ASK to THINK–TEL WHY" model, which was an inquiry-based model of reciprocal peer tutoring in which tutoring partners mediated each other's learning, supporting the distribution of cognition and metacognition to promote complex, higher-level learning. The article focused on what was being distributed during "ASK to THINK–TEL WHY" (i.e., the cognitive tasks of questioning, explaining, thinking, problem solving, monitoring and regulation of learning) and how these cognitions were distributed across the tutoring pair and various aspects of their learning environment. Research on the effectiveness of the model in classrooms showed that the model promoted students' construction of new knowledge.

Examining a completely different context, Breed et al. (2013) explored the use of self-directed metacognitive questioning in economically deprived rural schools in the KwaZulu-Natal provinces in South Africa. The study focused on five teachers and 99 grade 10 students in five schools. The teachers were trained to guide learners in the application of metacognitive regulation and the learners subsequently used metacognitive questions. Data gathering was through interviews with the teachers and student journals. Results indicated that the teachers viewed the implementation of the questions as difficult and time-consuming and that they found the learners to be either reluctant or unwilling to engage in questioning. However, the learners' journals indicated that the learners experienced the questions to be helpful in directing their thinking. This study is of interest in that it took place in an extremely deprived context and showed differences between teacher and student responses.

The effect of homework assignments enriched with metacognitive questions on students' mathematics achievement and homework behaviors was investigated by Özcan and Erktin (2015). A quasi-experimental design with pre- and post-test measures and two groups (experimental and control) was employed to investigate the effect of the enriched homework with 44 students. The students in the experimental group responded to metacognitive questions as they worked on homework that otherwise was common to both groups. Mathematics scores were used as a pre-test and post-test of mathematics achievement. The results revealed a significant difference between the mathematics scores of students who had been given homework assignments enriched with metacognitive questions and those who had not been given such homework.

Specimen Program

Researchers have identified constraints such as teacher domination, student passivity, peer pressures and institutional barriers that are likely to impede the student questioning process. Student questioning runs counter to normative conventions of classroom discourse and role relationships. In other words, teachers ask questions in class and students answer them. On the other hand, it has been argued that self-questioning is among the most potent cognitive strategies for stimulating learning, because question generation prompts learners to search for answers that they themselves want to know. Self-questioning is one of the most effective monitoring and regulating strategies of all the various metacognitive strategies.

Ciardiello (1998) developed an explicit instructional model to train students at an inner-city high school to raise questions at four different cognitive levels of thinking using three sequential stages: identification, categorization and construction of questions. She utilized a questioning taxonomy which categorized four types of questions: memory-based, convergent, divergent and evaluative.

Implementation

Initial Teacher Behaviors
Stage 1: Identifying divergent thinking questions
- Explain the purpose and value of asking questions in class.
- Introduce questioning strategy by establishing links between the initial process of identifying questions and the culminating process of generating questions.
- In a whole-class instruction format, explain the meaning of the term divergent by highlighting its open-ended and expansive nature.
- Review key words or question stems (provide cue cards) that can be associated with this questioning level, such as: "if … then …"; "suppose that …"; "imagine …"; " predict …".
- Offer review exercises in which students demonstrate ability to recognize divergent thinking questions from a pool of other types of cognitive questions. Direct students to underline or highlight the signal words.
- Offer immediate, corrective feedback.
- Move to the next phase of training when you assess that students are ready.

Stage 2: Classifying divergent thinking questions
- Explain how the process of classifying questions serves as a precondition for constructing questions.
- Provide an array of sample questions including those representing the four different cognitive types.
- Direct formation of categories of representative questions.

- Have students identify the common characteristics of the listed divergent questions.
- Provide review exercises.
- Signal transition to the next phase of questioning training.

Stage 3: Generating divergent thinking questions
- Model or demonstrate how to write divergent thinking questions from reading material (the author used primary and secondary source documents as well as political cartoons and photographs related to the topic of the Great Depression). Use think-aloud protocols.
- Direct students to construct divergent questions as they read while simulating teacher modeling.
- Review students' questions. Provide immediate corrective feedback. Use a whole-class format to answer students' questions.
- Summarize objectives of the training session.

Cue Cards for Question Types
Memory questions
Signal words: who, what, where, when?
Cognitive operations: naming, defining, identifying, designating, yes or no responses. Naming: What is a synonym for democracy?
Defining: Where is the 38th parallel in Korea?
Identifying: Who is Andrew Johnson?
Designating: When does the 21st century officially begin?
Yes or no: Are 18-year-olds allowed to vote in the U.S.?

Convergent thinking questions
Signal words/short question stems: why, how, in what ways?
Cognitive operations: explaining, stating relationships, comparing and contrasting.
Explaining: Why was U.S. President Andrew Johnson impeached?
Stating relationships: How was the invasion of Grenada a modern-day example of the Monroe Doctrine in action?

Comparing and contrasting: In what ways is the anti-apartheid movement in South Africa similar to the civil rights movement in the United States?

Divergent thinking questions
Signal words/short question stems: imagine, suppose, predict; If … then …? How might …? Can you create …? What are some possible consequences …?
Cognitive operations: predicting, hypothesizing, inferring, reconstructing.
Predicting: What predictions can you make regarding the budget surplus?
Hypothesizing: How might life have been different in the United States if the South had won the Civil War?
Inferring: What are some possible consequences of the fall of communism in Eastern Europe?
Reconstructing: Can you create a new amendment granting equal rights to women?

Evaluative thinking
Signal words/short question stems: defend, judge, justify; What do you think …? What is your opinion …?
Cognitive operations: valuing, judging, defending, justifying choices.
Valuing: How do you feel about abortion for teenagers?
Judging: What do you think of capital punishment for drug dealers?
Defending: Why did you vote for Bill Clinton?
Justifying choices: Why would you prefer to live in the suburbs?

Later Teacher Behaviors
Stage 1: Identifying divergent thinking questions
- Encourage students to establish the purpose and value of generating questions.
- Elicit reasons why the process of generating questions depends on ability to identify different cognitive levels of questions.

- Call on students to brainstorm the meaning of the term divergent questions.
- Encourage students to develop a list of signal words and phrases that could help in recognition of divergent questions.
- Organize the formation of small cooperative groups to work on review exercises with guided practice.
- Elicit feedback from students regarding transition to the next training phase or the need for additional review exercises.

Stage 2: Classifying divergent thinking questions

- Encourage students to explain how classifying questions can be useful as a learning event prior to generating questions.
- Provide an array of cognitive questions including a sample of divergent thinking questions.
- Encourage students to work together to categorize examples.
- Serve as coordinator or facilitator – review generated questions with students.
- Obtain student input regarding the need for extra review or movement to the next activity.

Stage 3: Generating divergent thinking questions

- Explain to students that they and you will take turns asking and answering divergent-type questions from selected reading material.
- Allow students to decide who will initiate the question modeling.
- Proceed to read and generate questions one paragraph at a time from the text.
- Help students formulate appropriate questions whenever difficulties emerge.
- Continue reciprocal questioning until students display that they know how to generate and answer divergent thinking questions.

- Encourage students to summarize the objectives of the three training stages of identifying, classifying, and constructing divergent thinking questions.

General Principles

The application of the initial and later teacher behaviors reflects that cognitive strategies occur in three separate but related stages. Each of the strategies follows the sequence of identifying, classifying and constructing questions. This division into small, manageable steps adheres to the findings of cognitive strategy research, which suggests that successful learning of new material occurs in reinforceable and incremental segments. In addition, making connections and associations among the thinking processes of identification, classification and generation consolidates the process of asking questions.

Modeling is an important part of the scaffolding procedure in both sets of teacher behaviors. In the first, the demonstration of student questioning procedure is teacher-centered. The teacher walks students through the various phases while vocalizing his/her thoughts. These think-alouds are a form of "mental modeling" as the teacher describes the reasoning process while performing an instructional action. In the latter version, the teacher and the students share the modeling of the question generation strategy.

One feature of metacognition is locus of control or the ability to assert independence in thinking and action. Students with low levels of independence will probably tend to prefer a structured questioning procedure such as is embodied in the initial teacher behaviors. The reverse process would conceivably work for the later teacher behaviors in which students take a more active role in generating questions (and are presumably in possession of a higher level of control). The autonomy afforded by the later teacher behaviors fosters self-regulated learning and provides for freedom of choice.

The independent practice phase can be accomplished in several different ways. It could take the form of teacher-led practice, or be accomplished independently with a routine of specific procedures guided by prompts such as checklists, or it could occur through student cooperative practice in small groups.

References

Breed, B., Mentz, E., Havenga, M., Govender, I., Govender, D., Dignum, F., & Dignum, V. (2013). Views of the use of self-directed metacognitive questioning during pair programming in economically deprived rural schools. *African Journal of Research in Mathematics, Science and Technology Education*, *17*(3), 206–219. http://dx.doi.org/10.1080/10288457.2013.839154

Ciardiello, A. V. (1998). Did you ask a good question today? Alternative cognitive and metacognitive strategies. *Journal of Adolescent & Adult Literacy*, *42*(3), 210–219. https://www.jstor.org/stable/40014681

Graesser, A. C., & Person, N. K. (1994). Question asking during tutoring. *American Educational Research Journal*, *31*(1), 104–137. https://doi.org/10.3102/00028312031001104

King, A. (1998). Transactive peer tutoring: Distributing cognition and metacognition. *Educational Psychology Review*, *10*, 57–74. https://doi.org/10.1023/A:1022858115001

Özcan, Z. Ç., & Erktin, E. (2015). Enhancing mathematics achievement of elementary school students through homework assignments enriched with metacognitive questions. *Eurasia Journal of Mathematics, Science & Technology Education*, *11*(6), 1415–1427. doi: 10.12973/eurasia.2015.1402a

Rosenshine, B., Meister, C., & Chapman, S. (1996). Teaching students to generate questions: A review of the intervention studies. *Review of Educational Research*, *66*(2), 181–221. https://doi.org/10.3102/00346543066002181

7
Summarizing

As early as 1981, Brown and her colleagues (Brown et al., 1981) noted that mature summarizers select only the most important information in the text and are able to condense it succinctly and coherently in their own words. In doing so, they depart systematically from the original wording and sequential organization of the text, combining information across paragraphs and rearranging it into topic clusters. In contrast, novice or "immature" summarizers (e.g., young children and poor readers) adopt a "copy-delete" strategy, simply deleting information they deem unnecessary and retaining text elements verbatim.

The writer's task in summary writing, then, is not only to originate and organize but to choose what to include, eliminate and reorganize. It is far more complex than simple recall. Summary writers need to be able to differentiate main ideas from supporting details and inconsequential information and then to transform the ideas into written discourse. The length of text and genre are important variables for summary writing. For beginning writers, text length is important because it affects the ability of the student to summarize. Children are also affected by genre – simple narratives are summarized more easily and naturally because they follow a chain of events, whereas expository texts are often more disjointed, making summaries more difficult.

Definition

Summarization is the act of expressing the most important facts or ideas about something or someone in a short and clear form and in an appropriate order, or a text in which these facts or ideas are expressed. A powerful tool for understanding organizing, and remembering information from texts, summarization embraces other activities such as identifying main ideas, distinguishing main ideas from supporting details, determining the structure and organization of the text and recognizing sequences of events. These activities are all crucial to good comprehension.

Background

The research literature on summarization is rather elderly and the topic seems to have become unfashionable with researchers. No review on summarization was discovered.

Random assignment of three forms of summarization instruction comprised the treatment and control conditions explored in a study (Bean & Steenwyk, 1984) of 60 sixth-grade students in three classes. The two treatment groups received direct instruction in either a rule-governed approach to summarization or an intuitive approach. A control group simply received advice to find main ideas with no explicit modeling. Two dependent measures were used to judge the efficacy of the three instructional approaches to summarization: (a) a paragraph summary writing task, and (b) a standardized test of paragraph comprehension. On both measures, both treatment groups significantly outperformed the control group.

Kurtz and Borkowski (1985) examined relationships between metamemory (the awareness and control people have over their memory operations) and strategic behavior in 130 impulsive or reflective children in the fourth, fifth and sixth grades. At pretraining, children were assessed on metamemory, cognitive tempo, summarization skills and teacher ratings of impulsive behavior in the classroom. Children in three experimental groups then received prose summarization instructions, summarization instructions in conjunction with metacognitive training about the importance of a reflective approach to learning, or no instructions. Following training, children were again measured on tempo, summarization skills and teacher ratings of impulsivity. Analyses of academic strategy use indicated superior performance for children who had received both summarization and metacognitive training. Causal modeling analyses showed early metamemory as a causal antecedent of later strategy acquisition. This highlighted the dual importance of metacognitive knowledge as a precursor of later strategy acquisition and metacognitive skills as the "executor" for lower-level strategies.

Summarization training has been found to improve written summaries and also to have transfer effects to measures of reading comprehension, as well as making children more aware of the structure of ideas within text and of how individual ideas relate to each other. Participants in the study of Rinehart et al. (1986) were 70 sixth-grade students in two elementary schools. Direct instruction was followed by self-control training, in which students were taught not only a procedure, but also explicitly how to monitor, check and evaluate their use of that procedure. This was implemented by phasing out teacher direction and phasing in student control over the process during the course of the treatment. The phasing-out was reflected in the materials, which progressed from short paragraphs with typographical prompts, in the first session, to passages taken directly from content area materials, with no explicit prompts, by the end of the training. Four summarization operations were directly taught: (1) Identifying/selecting main information, (2) Deleting trivial information, (3) Deleting redundant information, (4) Relating main and important supporting information. The training improved recall of major but not minor information on a studying task. Path analyses showed that the summarization training affected recall of major information indirectly, through its effect on the amount of major information in students' notes, confirming a metacognitive hypothesis. The training also improved summaries of paragraphs that had main ideas stated within the paragraphs, but not those in which the statement of main ideas had to be invented. These results indicated that summarization training was an effective tool.

Turning to digital technology, and in particular to automation of the process of assessing student writing, the computer tutor Summary Street provides feedback on students' written summaries (Caccamise et al., 2007). Graphically presented feedback guides this process to ensure adequate content coverage within given length constraints and the avoidance of redundant, irrelevant, overly detailed or plagiarized information. The experimental findings among middle school students showed not only improved summary writing when using the tool, but also transfer to independent summary writing. Students who practiced summarizing without guidance did not perform as well. Moreover, Summary Street users also scored higher on comprehension test items that required gist-level understanding.

More recently, increasingly sophisticated computer tools have emerged to support summarization. For example, QuillBot is an application which uses artificial intelligence to provide paraphrasing and summarization.

Specimen Program

Armbruster et al. (1987) noted that one approach to teaching text structure is to teach readers to use typographical cues (headings, subheadings and paragraphs) as indices of text structure. This hierarchical summarization consists of first preparing a skeletal outline based on headings, subheadings and paragraphs, and then writing a main idea statement for every point on the outline. Students who completed hierarchical summaries tended to outperform control groups on some kinds of dependent measures. However, a limitation of the strategy is that it is highly dependent on the heading-subheading organizational format and on the ability of the headings and subheadings to convey the structure of the text.

Nonetheless, in their own study, Armbruster and colleagues gave fifth-grade students instruction on a conventional expository text structure (including instruction on summarizing) to see how it would affect their ability to comprehend expository text having this structure. Instruction for the experimental group focused on a problem/solution structure, an organizational pattern commonly found in social studies textbooks. Expository prose with this structure conveys information about a problem that an individual or group encounters, how they attempt to solve the problem and the results of the attempt to solve the problem. In the study, children were taught not only to recognize the problem/solution structure, but also to use it in organizing their own written summaries of what they had read. Structure training was compared with the more traditional practice of asking students questions and discussing the answers after reading.

The major hypothesis was that instruction in the problem/solution structure would facilitate the formation of a macrostructure for text with a problem/solution structure. Therefore, compared to the traditionally trained group, the structure-trained group should (a) recall more information on an essay (probed recall) test over the passage main idea, (b) recall about the same amount of information on a short-answer test over specific information not necessarily included in the macrostructure, (c) write summaries that included more passage main ideas, and (d) write better organized summaries (i.e., summaries that had a recognizable structure). An additional hypothesis was that using the problem/solution text structure as an organizational framework for classroom discussion should facilitate students' retention of the content discussed.

Thus, fifth-grade students were instructed in a particular text structure to see whether it would improve their ability to learn from similarly structured social studies material. Eighty-two students were assigned either to a structure training group, which received direct instruction in recognizing and summarizing a conventional text structure (problem/solution), or to a traditional training group, which read and discussed answers to questions about social studies passages. As measured by responses to a main idea essay question and by written summaries of two passages, students' ability to abstract the macrostructure of problem/solution text read independently was improved by the structure training.

Implementation

"Workbooks" were prepared for both the structure training and the traditional groups. The booklets for the structure training subjects contained (a) a definition and description of the problem/solution text structure along with a schematic representation (frame) of the problem/solution text structure; (b) explicit rules for how to write a summary of problem/solution passages, including a pattern for writing and guidelines for checking the summary; (c) 13 problem/solution passages from fourth- and fifth-grade social studies textbooks, ranging in length from 100 to 500 words; and (d) multiple copies of problem/solution frames accompanied by blank lines for students to use in writing their summaries of the passages.

Here is the "frame":

How to Summarize Problem/Solution Passages

    Sentence 1 – Tells who had a problem and what the problem is.
    Sentence 2 – Tells what action was taken to try to solve the problem.
    Sentence 3 – Tells what happened as a result of the action taken.

Pattern for Writing a Summary of a Problem/Solution Passage

_____ had a problem because _____
_____.
Therefore _____.
As a result _____.

Guidelines for Checking Summaries of Problem/Solution Passages
    Check to see that:

1. Your summary has all of the information that should be in a summary of a problem/solution passage. Compare your summary with the original problem/solution passage to make sure your summary is accurate and complete.
2. You have used complete sentences.

3. The sentences are tied together with good connecting words.
4. The grammar and spelling are correct.

Each passage was accompanied by five questions. The questions were similar to those at the end of textbook lessons or chapters. Some of the questions were about information critical to the problem/solution structure; thus, they tapped information similar to that which would be discussed in the structure training group. For example, the question "What did Governor Clinton decide to do?" asks about the action taken to solve a problem. Other questions tapped particular facts in the passage that were not critical to the problem/solution structure, as in the question "What two cities were connected by the National Road when it was completed?" Each question was accompanied by four blank lines for answers.

Both the structure training and the traditional group were instructed in their normal classrooms with the regular teachers present. The instruction took place over 11 consecutive school days, for 45 minutes per day per class. The instruction for the structure training subjects followed principles of explicit or direct instruction. That is, the instruction featured teacher modeling of explicitly defined procedures, plenty of guided practice on increasingly longer and more difficult passages, teacher monitoring with corrective feedback, and independent practice.

Day 1. A rationale was provided for the project (i.e., that social studies texts discuss many problems and solutions; so, learning about problem/solution structures would help students focus on main ideas and remember important information). Using the first example of a problem/solution text in the workbook, the students discussed answers to the questions "Who has a problem?" "What is the problem?" "What actions were taken to solve the problem?" and "What were the results of those actions?" It was explained that these four questions were always associated with problem/solution texts. Then the problem/solution frame was introduced and students were told the diagram would help them organize answers to the four problem/solution questions. How answers to discussion questions could be recorded in the frame was demonstrated. Students filled out the frame in their workbooks.

Day 2. A brief review was conducted, which then led to a discussion of the second passage in the workbook, recording answers to problem/solution questions in a frame on the blackboard. It was explained to students that one way to learn from reading textbooks was to summarize the information. The guidelines for summarizing problem/solution passages were explained and modeled. Writing and checking summaries were based on the two passages already "framed" in the workbook. A discussion of the third workbook passage was then introduced, recording information in a frame on the blackboard. A summary was elicited from the class and recorded on the board. The class used the guidelines to check the summary; then the students copied the summary into their workbooks.

Days 3–9. Students continued to work consecutively through the workbook, following three steps for each passage: first, they read the passage silently, looking for information to answer the problem/solution questions; then they recorded notes on the passage in the provided problem/solution frames; finally, they wrote a summary of the framed information. Students gradually assumed greater independence in the last two steps. As students worked independently in their workbooks, the teacher circulated and monitored individual work, providing corrective feedback and assistance as needed. Students also were reminded to check their own summaries using the provided guidelines. After students had independently framed and summarized each passage, two or three of them were asked to write their frames and/or summaries on the board. (Sometimes they gave the summaries orally.) The class then discussed and provided feedback on the efforts. By the end of Day 9, all passages in the workbook had been read, framed and summarized.

Days 10–11. Students returned to their classroom textbook, to the place where regular social studies instruction had stopped prior to the intervention. Discussion after silent reading was organized around the problem/solution frame. The discussion points were recorded in a frame on the blackboard; then students summarized the frame orally.

An alternative structure for training summarization skills is given below:

Ask yourself, "What was the text about?" What did the writer say?"
Try to say the general theme to yourself.
LOOK BACK.
Reread the text to make sure you got the theme right.
Also reread to make sure that you really understand what the important parts of the text are.
Star important parts.

NOW USE THE FOUR RULES FOR WRITING A SUMMARY:

1. COLLAPSE LISTS. If you see a list of things, try to think of a word or phrase name for the whole list. For example, if you saw a list like "tête", "yeux", "bras", "mains", "jambes", and "pieds", you could say "body parts" (parties du corps). Or if you saw a list like "ski de fond", "ski de piste", "patinage sur glace", or "hockey", you could say "winter sports" (sports d'hiver).
2. USE TOPIC SENTENCES. Often authors write a sentence that summarizes a whole paragraph. It is called a topic sentence. If the author gives you one, you can use it in your summary. Unfortunately, not all paragraphs contain topic sentences. That means you may have to make up one for yourself. If you don't see a topic sentence, make up one of your own.
3. GET RID OF UNNECESSARY DETAIL. Some text information can be repeated in a passage. In other words, the same thing can be said in a number of different ways, all in one passage. Other text information can be unimportant or trivial. Since summaries are meant to be short, get rid of repetitive or trivial information.
4. COLLAPSE PARAGRAPHS. Paragraphs are often related to one another. Some paragraphs explain one or more other paragraphs. Some paragraphs just expand on the information presented in other paragraphs. Some paragraphs

are more necessary than other paragraphs. Decide which paragraphs should be kept or gotten rid of, and which might be joined together.

CHECK YOUR SUMMARY RETHINK:

Reread a paragraph of the text.
Try to say the theme of that paragraph to yourself.
Is the theme a topic sentence?
Have you underlined it?
Or is the topic sentence missing?
If it is missing, have you written one in the margin?

CHECK AND DOUBLE-CHECK:

Did you leave in any lists?
Did you skip anything?
Is all the important information in the summary?

A FINAL SUGGESTION + POLISH THE SUMMARY.

When a lot of information is reduced from an original passage, the resulting concentrated information often sounds very unnatural. Fix this problem and create a more natural sounding summary. Adjustments may include, but are not limited to: paraphrasing, the insertion of connecting words like "and" or "because", and the insertion of introductory or closing statements. Paraphrasing is especially useful here because it improves your ability to remember the material.

References

Armbruster, B. B., Anderson, T. H., & Ostertag, J. (1987). Does text structure/summarization instruction facilitate learning from expository text? *Reading Research Quarterly*, *22*(3), 331–346. https://doi.org/10.2307/747972

Bean, T. W., & Steenwyk, F. L. (1984). The effect of three forms of summarization instruction on sixth graders' summary writing and comprehension. *Journal of Reading Behavior*, *16*(4), 297–306. https://doi.org/10.1080/10862968409547523

Brown, A. L., Campione, J. C., & Day, J. D. (1981). Learning to learn: On training students to learn from texts. *Educational Researcher*, *10*(2), 14–21. https://doi.org/10.3102/0013189X010002014

Caccamise, D., Franzke, M., Eckhoff, A., Kintsch, E., & Kintsch, W. (2007). Guided practice in technology-based summary writing. In D. S. McNamara (Ed.), *Reading Comprehension Strategies: Theories, Interventions, and Technologies* (pp. 375–396). Mahwah: Lawrence Erlbaum.

Kurtz, B. E., & Borkowski, J. G. (1985). *Metacognition and the development of strategic skills in impulsive and reflective children*. Paper presented at the biennial meeting of the Society for Research in Child Development (Toronto, Ontario, Canada, April 25–28, 1985). ERIC number ED 257 572.

Rinehart, S. D., Stahl, S. A., & Erickson, L. G. (1986). Some effects of summarization training on reading and studying. *Reading Research Quarterly*, *21*(4), 422–438. https://www.jstor.org/stable/747614

8

Modeling

There are two meanings of modeling. One is that teachers do skilled "metacognitive work" (either consciously or subconsciously) and bringing this work into the forefront of teachers' reflective awareness allows them to model the "how" of metacognition to students still developing those skills, showing or demonstrating specific procedures to follow for using a strategy and explaining the usefulness of the strategy. As teachers act as models, they also verbalize what they are doing, why they are doing it and ways for overcoming obstacles. They also signal what they think is important by what they leave in and what they leave out. However, the second meaning of modeling refers to creating abstract representations of the real world used to aid understanding, which is the meaning defined below.

Definition

Models are systematically constructed simplified representations of physical systems, used to describe, represent and explain the mechanisms underlying physical phenomena. Modeling is about building conceptual representations or analogies of things which exist in the real world. A model is an abstraction, which allows people to concentrate on the essentials of a (complex) problem by keeping out non-essential details and at the same time showing how important variables interact and in what sequence. For example, a road map is a model of a particular part of the earth's surface which omits many details because they are not relevant to the map's purpose. Models are subject to change and require repeated testing so that a model can maintain or improve its correspondence with reality. There are two different kinds of models: static models, which describe a set of elements and any relationships that exist between them; and dynamic models, which describe the behavior of one or more elements over time.

Background

Harrison and Treagust (2000) developed a typology of nine varieties of models typically used in teaching and learning. These included scale models, which demonstrate external shapes, colors and textures of a system, as well as pedagogical analogical models, which are models in which some feature of the system is either simplified or exaggerated. Pedagogical analogical models include symbolic models, such as chemical formulas; mathematical models, such as equations and graphs; theoretical models, used to explain theoretical relationships; maps, diagrams, and tables, which visualize patterns and relationships; concept-process models, which can include multiple complex abstract processes; and simulations, including dynamic online simulations. Pedagogical analogical models can vary in abstractness and complexity, but all are designed to help a student develop their mental model. In general, Harrison and Treagust suggested that because students often focus on surface-level features of models and do not always understand what teachers are intending to convey, teachers not only need to demonstrate how to use models in class, they also need to present a variety of models of the same phenomenon and make sure students are involved in negotiating the meanings of a model.

Modeling theory was further developed and reviewed by Jørgensen and Fath (2011), who discussed model components as well as modeling steps, which included model conceptualization, mathematical formulation, parameter estimation and calibration, sensitivity analysis and validation. Many different model types with different advantages and disadvantages were available. Various methods were presented to select models. To choose among these required sound scientific constraints.

Kistner et al. (2010) noted that teachers could promote self-regulated learning either directly by teaching learning strategies or indirectly by arranging a learning environment that enabled students to practice self-regulation. This study investigated teachers' direct and indirect promotion of self-regulated learning and its relation to the development of students' performance. Twenty mathematics teachers and 538 grade 9 students were videotaped for a three-lesson unit on the Pythagorean theorem. Students' mathematics performance was tested several times before and after the observed lessons. A coding system was used to assess teachers' implicit or explicit instruction of cognitive strategies (e.g., organization), metacognitive strategies (e.g., planning) and motivational strategies (e.g., resource management). Ratings were used to assess features of the learning environment that fostered self-regulation. Results revealed that much strategy teaching took place in an implicit way, while explicit strategy teaching and supportive learning environment were rare. The instruction of organization strategies and some features of the learning environment (constructivism, transfer) related positively to students' performance development. In contrast to implicit strategy instruction, explicit strategy instruction was associated with a gain in performance. These results revealed a discrepancy between the usefulness of explicit strategy instruction and its rare occurrence in the classroom.

Focusing now on a number of more specific empirical papers, Panaoura et al. (2009) developed an intervention program dependent on a mathematical model and investigated the improvement in students' self-representation of their self-regulatory performance in mathematics. Three tools were constructed for pre- and post-test, administered to 255 students (11 years old). The mathematical model was presented to students as a useful tool for problem solving through a web page. Results confirmed that providing students with the opportunity to self-monitor their learning behavior through the use of modeling when they encountered obstacles in problem solving was one possible way to enhance students' self-regulation.

Most of the studies of modeling are in mathematics and science, but Sarimanah (2016) applied one model to reading comprehension – the metacognitive Preview, Question, Read, Reflect, Recite, Review (PQ4R) strategy-based model. With experimental and control groups, the results showed that the metacognitive PQ4R model was effective in improving students' reading ability.

Vorhölter (2018) examined metacognitive knowledge and strategies for individuals working on modeling problems as compared to whole groups. The structure of metacognitive strategies used by 431 grade 9 students was analyzed. Results revealed the same structure for metacognitive strategies at individual and at group level. These metacognitive strategies could be differentiated into strategies ensuring a smooth modeling process, strategies for regulating when problems occur, and strategies for evaluating the whole modeling process.

Specimen Program

Wade-Jaimes et al. (2018) noted that modeling is considered an important scientific practice and modeling instruction has the potential to support conceptual change in students in physics. However, when students are not taught how to think about modeling, or how to develop and use models, the learning potential of modeling may be limited. This study argued that the use and explicit teaching of metacognitive tools was likely to increase students' ability to use and make sense of models. This study was conducted with 45 African-American girls in the twelfth grade (ages 16–18) from an all-girls high school situated in a large urban school district in the southeastern United States.

A sequence of activities which incorporated metacognitive tools such as interactive questioning and individual reflection was used with a variety of models (mental, physical, simulated and mathematical) in a physics unit of electricity. Using data from classroom observations, individual student reflections, group-created posters and classroom discussion, evidence was found to demonstrate the complicated nature of conceptual change, the importance of using a variety of different representations (models) of a phenomenon and the critical role of the teacher in learning. Teachers needed to be aware of these processes and able to give students the time needed to fully explore and develop multiple models, and support to think critically about models. Although many classrooms were limited in time, this process was seen as necessary to move beyond rote memorization toward meaningful conceptual change.

Implementation

It is important to note that the students in this study had previously engaged in many inquiry-oriented activities and were expected to investigate and share their findings with the rest of the class on a regular basis. Most of the learning activities in the class throughout the year involved whole-class construction of knowledge rather than traditional lectures and note-taking. The teacher encouraged open communication and sharing, valuing all students' contributions. Because of this, students were comfortable sharing their observations.

During this learning cycle, students engaged in a sequence of model-based learning activities, interspersed with group and whole-class discussion, individual reflections, and group poster construction. The sequence and purpose of the activities was as follows (Title of activity: Purpose: Data collected and metacognitive tools):

1. Probe: Elicit students' current understanding of electricity: Students choose one other student to agree with and explain their choice, students are assigned to groups with students who chose different answers to foster discussion and debate, groups discuss their selections and record group thoughts on a poster.
2. Initial poster: Groups create a visual representation of their initial thoughts.

3. Initial physical model: Test students' initial predictions about the circuit, students collect concrete observations: Students replicate system shown in the probe to test initial prediction, groups record their observations on their posters, teacher leads class discussion.
4. Poster update: Elicit group understanding of electricity: Groups add new information to their posters and evaluate prior information.
5. Reflection 1: Elicit students' current understanding of electricity: Students complete written reflection individually to indicate if the group discussion or physical model has changed their thinking.
6. Second physical model: Students continue to test initial predictions: Based on class discussion, students use additional wires, light bulbs and batteries to explore variations of the physical model, groups record their observations on their posters, teacher leads class discussion.
7. Poster update: Elicit group understanding of electricity: Groups add new information to their posters and evaluate new information.
8. Reflection 2: Elicit students' current understanding of electricity: Students complete written reflection individually to indicate if the class discussion or second physical model has changed their mind.
9. Analogy: Provide a concrete system to visualize the abstract concept of the direction of current flow: Teacher presents the analogy of a water system to provide a concrete example of current flow as well as introducing relevant vocabulary (current, voltage, resistance).
10. Simulation: Visualize the flow of electrons within the circuit and how the flow changes when the circuit changes: Students build circuits using the simulation and observe what happens when they change the current and the voltage in the circuit, groups record their observations on their posters, teacher leads class discussion.
11. Poster update: Elicit group understanding of electricity: Groups add new information to their posters and evaluate prior information.

12. Reflection 3: Elicit students' current understanding of electricity: Individual students complete written reflection to indicate if the analogy and/or simulation has changed their thinking.
13. Mathematical model: Derive mathematical relationship between current, voltage and resistance: Students use data collected during the simulation to create a graph of voltage vs. current, teacher leads a discussion on interpreting the graph to derive Ohm's law.
14. Final reflection: Elicit students' current understanding of electricity: Individual students complete written reflection describing how their understanding of electricity has changed since the probe.

During the class discussions, each group described what they had observed and what they could reason from their observations, then the teacher led a discussion, providing guidance through probing questions that were designed to enhance students' metacognition and foster conceptual change. Probing questions designed to support the intelligibility of a concept generally began, "What did you see …?" or "Can you give an example of …?" Probing questions designed to support the plausibility of a concept generally began, "How can you use that to explain …?" or "Does that agree with what you saw when …?" Probing questions designed to support the fruitfulness of a concept generally began, "What do you predict will happen when you …?"

The overall target concepts were that current flows constantly in one direction throughout a series circuit and the given relationships between current, voltage, and resistance (i.e., Ohm's law). In the first activity, students constructed a simple, physical circuit. This provided students with an example of the phenomenon under study, current electricity, and also provided many of the benefits of a physical model. Students were able to manipulate the circuit by rearranging, adding, or subtracting the components, and observe the result. Students engaged in this physical exploration twice: once with the initial circuit and again with additional tools to manipulate the circuit. The learning goal of this activity was for students to observe that similar lights in a series circuit have similar brightness. Students also observed that adding more lights to a circuit caused all lights to dim, and adding more batteries caused all lights to brighten.

From a conceptual change perspective, interacting with the working circuit first provided a discrepant event leading to disequilibrium for students who expected the bulbs to be of different brightness. Observing that different iterations of the circuit, i.e., with additional bulbs or batteries, also had equally bright bulbs increased the intelligibility of the concepts that current is the same throughout a series circuit, that increased voltage increases current in a series circuit and that increased resistance decreases voltage in a series circuit. (However, students did not yet have this terminology to describe their observations.) The teacher used class discussion and probing questions to increase the status of these concepts by asking, for example, "What did you see in the circuit? What happened when you added more light bulbs?" Although these questions seem simple, they prompted students to make sense of what they observed, give an example of the concept and explain it to others in the class, all of which indicated intelligibility of a concept.

Next, students were presented with an analogy comparing a circuit to a water system. This provided students with a concrete way to visualize current flow and was also used to introduce relevant vocabulary, such as current, voltage, and resistance, and connect these terms to the physical exploration. The teacher first drew a closed set of pipes in a square on the board. She told the students that the pipes were an analogy for the wires in their circuits. Students identified that something would be needed to "push" the water to get it circulating. The teacher then added a pump to the drawing on the board, asking students what it might represent in a circuit (a battery), and introducing the term "voltage". Next, students identified that the water represented the electrons in the circuit. The teacher introduced the term "current" to describe the flow of electric charge through a wire, similar to the flow of water through the pipes. She asked students if it was possible that the water could move in one part of the system but not the others and students agreed that would not be possible.

Finally, the teacher asked the students what they could use in the analogy to represent the light bulbs in their circuits. Although this was more difficult for many students, some students volunteered that it would need to be something that used the energy from the water to do something. The teacher suggested a water wheel and added one to the drawing on the board, introducing the term "resistance" as something that uses the energy from an electric circuit, slowing down the flow of charge. Then, using the analogy and drawing on the board, the teacher asked the students to revisit the question of the direction of flow of current in a series circuit. She asked, "If our water analogy accurately represents a circuit, does the water/current flow in one direction or two directions?" Students identified that the water would have to flow out of the pump in one direction through the pipes. The purpose of this discussion was to introduce the terminology to students, but also to give them a way to make sense of how the current flows in a circuit, i.e., to make the unidirectional flow of current intelligible.

The analogy also provided a link to a simulated model, which allowed students to manipulate voltage and resistance in an online circuit and observe the changes in the current. The purpose of the simulation was to provide students with a way to observe more abstract features of circuits, such as the flow of electrons, which they could then use to explain their observations during the physical observation. Before using the simulation, the teacher and students discussed the benefits (i.e., visualizing a phenomenon that is not physically observable, collecting data for calculations) and drawbacks (choosing one visualization may limit consideration of other possible models) of using an online simulation.

From a conceptual change perspective, the analogy and simulation increased the plausibility of the concept of constant current throughout the circuit. The teacher used probing questions to prompt students to integrate this new information into their existing conceptual ecologies around electricity. For example, she asked students to not only describe what they saw in the simulation, but also apply it to the physical circuits they had created. When the idea seemed plausible to students, in that they indicated they believed in the concept and could use it to explain other observations, she again used probing questions to increase the fruitfulness of the concept. For example, she asked students to predict what would happen to the current, voltage and resistance (qualitatively) when the circuit was adjusted. Additionally, students used the simulation to collect data that were then used to construct a mathematical model, deriving Ohm's law. This also increased the fruitfulness of the concepts as students were able to use the relationship between current, voltage and resistance to make quantitative predictions about the circuit.

At the beginning of the learning cycle, students were given a probe showing an electric circuit with two light bulbs connected to it. In the probe, there are five statements: three of which represent common alternate conceptions about current electricity, one statement represents the accepted scientific conception, and one statement indicates that none of the statements are correct. The students were asked to choose one statement that they agreed with and provide explanation-based reasoning for why they agreed with it. This probe was revisited five times throughout the sequence of learning activities and students were asked if their answer had changed and why.

Students were also asked to answer reflective assessment questions provided by the teacher after each phase of the learning cycle, to reflect not only on what they had learned but also how they learned it. The students were specifically asked to reflect on how each activity related to prior activities and make connections between the various types of models. Questions included, "Which opinion did you originally agree with/agree with yesterday? Do you still agree with that? What did you see or do in class to support that answer? What did you see or do in class that supports your new answer?" Explicit metacognitive questioning such as "Why do you think that?" and "How does that relate to the circuit you built/analogy/simulation?" was used to elicit student reasoning. Answers provided on these reflections were used to evaluate the depth of student understanding.

Students were assigned to groups based on their initial responses to the probe. Each group consisted of students with different reasoning supporting claims from the probe. The group posters were intended to capture groups' evolving understanding of circuits, as artifacts representing their mental models.

This activity began during students' initial group discussion and continued after each learning activity until the end of the sequence of activities. Groups were instructed to negotiate new information and to decide what information warranted inclusion on the poster.

References

Harrison, A. G., & Treagust, D. F. (2000). A typology of school science models. *International Journal of Science Education*, *22*(9), 1011–1026. doi: 10.1080/095006900416884

Jørgensen, S. E., & Fath, B. D. (2011). Concepts of modelling. In S. E. Jørgensen & B. D. Fath (Eds.), *Developments in Environmental Modelling*, *23*, 19–93. London: Elsevier. https://doi.org/10.1016/B978-0-444-53567-2.00002-8

Kistner, S., Rakoczy, K., Otto, B., Dignath-van Ewijk, C., Büttner, G., & Klieme, E. (2010). Promotion of self-regulated learning in classrooms: Investigating frequency, quality, and consequences for student performance. *Metacognition and Learning*, *5*, 157–171. doi: 10.1007/s11409-010-9055-3

Panaoura, A., Gagatsis, A., & Demetriou, A. (2009). An intervention to the metacognitive performance: Self-regulation in mathematics and mathematical modeling. *Acta Didactica Universitatis Comenianae Mathematics*, *9*, 63–79.

Sarimanah, E. (2016). Effectiveness of PQ4R metacognitive strategy-based reading learning models in junior high school. *International Journal of Language Education and Culture Review*, *2*(1), 74–81. doi: 10.21009/IJLECR.021.08

Vorhölter, K. (2018). Conceptualization and measuring of metacognitive modelling competencies: Empirical verification of theoretical assumptions. *ZDM – Mathematics Education*, *50*, 343–354. https://doi.org/10.1007/s11858-017-0909-x

Wade-Jaimes, K., Demir, K., & Qureshi, A. (2018). Modeling strategies enhanced by metacognitive tools in high school physics to support student conceptual trajectories and understanding of electricity. *Science Education*, *102*, 711–743. doi: 10.1002/sce.21444

9

Predictions

Prediction skills enable children to metacognitively anticipate task difficulties, making them work steadily on difficult tasks and faster on easier tasks. Furthermore, prediction skills enable children to associate certain problems with other problems, to develop intuitive knowledge about the conditions required for carrying out a task and to distinguish between apparent and actual difficulties in problem solving.

Definition

A prediction is what someone thinks will happen in the future – "to tell beforehand". "Pre" means "before" and "diction" has to do with talking. So, a prediction is a statement about the future. It is often a guess, sometimes based on facts or evidence, but not always. Synonyms for prediction are forecast, foretell, prognosticate and prophesy.

Background

An early study by Nolan (1991) looked at the effectiveness of combining two cognitive strategies: self-questioning and prediction. Forty-two students in grades 6, 7 and 8 with reading comprehension below grade level were matched and assigned randomly to one of three groups: self-questioning with prediction, self-questioning, and control vocabulary intervention. The self-questioning with prediction group scored higher on reading comprehension than the others.

A study to assess metacognitive skills that preceded or followed task engagement, rather than the processes that occurred during a task, was undertaken by Garrett et al. (2006), who examined prediction and evaluation skills among children with (n = 17) or without (n = 179) mathematics learning disability from grades 2–4. Children were asked to predict which of several mathematical problems they could solve correctly. Thirty minutes later, they were asked to solve similar problems. From third to fourth grade, there was an increase in the proportion of calculations that students predicted they could solve; more for students without mathematical difficulties.

Desoete (2009) conducted a two-year longitudinal study with 66 children in grades 3 and 4 from two primary schools, using the computerized Evaluation and Prediction Assessment. In this evaluation, children were asked to look at exercises without solving them and to predict on a four-point rating scale whether they would be successful in this task. Half of the children were trained in grade 3 in the metacognitive skill of predicting their abilities in solving mathematics tasks. The intervention took place in the classroom five times in two weeks, 50 minutes each time. All children completed pre and post mathematics tests. Children in the metacognitive condition had higher prediction and evaluation skills after the training (effect size partial eta-squared = 0.17, large) and gained higher arithmetic reasoning scores than the children in the control condition (effect size partial eta-squared = 0.71, very large). Thus, there was progress in metacognition and in mathematics skills and children in the metacognitive group did better than children in the control group.

Research has shown that better readers demonstrate more metacognitive knowledge than poor readers and that reading ability improves through strategy instruction. The study of Furnes and Norman (2015) compared three forms of metacognition in dyslexic (n = 22) versus normally developing readers (n = 22). Participants read two factual texts, with learning outcomes measured by a memory task. Mean ratings of predictions of performance and judgments of learning were lower in dyslexic readers, but dyslexic reading and spelling problems were not generally associated with lower levels of metacognitive knowledge or strategies.

Soto et al. (2019) explored relations between reading comprehension performance and self-reported components of metacognition in 87 grade 7–8 students from four schools in Chile (two public and two private schools). They read a science text and then made predictions about how they would perform on a comprehension test. Students' meta-comprehension accuracy was related to their performance at different levels of understanding. Students' text-based question performance accounted for significant variance in meta-comprehension accuracy for text-based questions and inference-based question performance accounted for significant variance in meta-comprehension accuracy for inference-based questions. This suggested that metacognitive and meta-comprehension knowledge was aligned with the level of information in text and was related to deeper understanding of texts.

Specimen Program

The development of the metacognitive skill of prediction was explored with deaf students in a middle school social studies classroom (Brigham & Hartman, 2010) – a particularly challenging population. The study used a qualitative action research design in which teachers collected observation data by directly observing the students and the classroom teacher before and during the intervention. The participants were five members (four boys and one girl aged 12 to 13½ years) of a combined sixth- and seventh-grade class at a school for the deaf. All were severely to profoundly deaf. All of the students were Hispanic and had parents who only spoke Spanish at home. None of the parents had learned sign language.

After observation of this group of learners and assessment of current skills, a unit was developed that integrated the teaching of prediction into their study of the American Revolution. It was found that these students were already using some metacognitive skills in their social studies class, but through direct instruction they were able to make more and better predictions related to the content being studied.

Four strategies were employed for teaching social studies to students who were deaf or hard of hearing: (a) using a time line, (b) teaching the meaning of prediction in a constructivist manner, (c) repeatedly reviewing the concept of prediction in multiple contexts, and (d) having students compare situations in their own lives with the ones in the historical events they were learning about.

Prediction was to be the one metacognitive skill taught during the intervention, because it could offer applications and practice within the students' current social studies content and could be easily practiced across academic subjects. Prediction questions were asked every day during the intervention. After each prediction, how well the students had done with their prediction was assessed. Consideration was given to whether the next prediction question should be at the same level of difficulty or entail a more complex prediction. The students' answers to the prediction questions were used to assess the effectiveness of the intervention.

By the end of the intervention, the students had all evidenced some understanding of the meaning of prediction and showed some ability to make predictions. The data reported in the form of student responses stood as evidence and was supported by interpretation of the students' positive body language and facial expressions, and their enthusiasm about responding during the interaction parts of the unit.

The study demonstrated how the social studies curriculum provided an opportunity for students to learn and implement metacognitive skills that helped them to understand the cause-and-effect relationships in history and eventually to become more active readers during a reading task.

Implementation

First, a time line was displayed in the classroom throughout the intervention period. It focused exclusively on events the students had just learned about (e.g., the First Continental Congress, the Boston Massacre and the Boston Tea Party) and those they were about to study (e.g., the Second Constitutional Convention, the colonists' presentation of the Olive Branch Petition to King George III, the appearance of Thomas Paine's pamphlet Common Sense and the writing and signing of the Declaration of Independence). The time line showed the year, the name of the event and an image representing either the event or the relevant document. At the start of every lesson, students used the time line to review everything they had previously learned. Later in the unit, students were asked to predict what happened next.

Second, the meaning of prediction was taught in a constructivist manner. For example, on the first day of the teaching unit, the students were shown the written word and sign PREDICT and were asked what they knew about the word (words that were signed in American Sign Language are displayed in all-uppercase letters, while words that were signed and spoken are displayed in quotes, without uppercasing). As the students answered, the teacher wrote each word on the board. None of the students knew the meaning of the word predict. However, all suggestions (e.g., LOOK, SEE, EYE) were signs that focused around the eyes and most had the movements away from the face, even though the sign EYE does not have movement away from the face. Because the sign for prediction is similar to the signs for look, see and eye, students were able to grasp the concept of prediction rather easily. Working together, the students and the teacher crafted a preliminary definition of prediction as "looking into the future and thinking about what might happen" after the students had each provided suggestions of what prediction meant.

Third, the repeated review of content happened with multiple academic topics as well as in nonacademic situations. For example, on the third day of the teaching unit, the students were studying digestion and were learning the steps and general process of digestion in science. The students were asked to make a prediction in response to the question "What happens when your body is finished with the food?" The students then did an experiment in which they mixed water (representing saliva) with apple slices to see what happened. At the end of the experiment the apple turned a brownish color, demonstrating how food changes color in the human body. Students were then asked to predict how the food they ate became a different color. Finally, while they were watching a Magic School Bus movie on digestion, students were asked to predict whether the gum that the main character had swallowed would stay in his body forever. Throughout the study, the students were asked to make predictions in relation to multiple academic topics as well as in non-academic situations to increase the likelihood that they would master the skill and generalize it.

Fourth, students were encouraged to compare situations in their own lives with ones in the historical events they were studying. From the initial observation, the teacher noticed that students were able to identify similarities between two items. Therefore, she directly taught them to make comparisons to analogous situations in their own lives to predict how people may have reacted to an event.

Here are some sample prediction questions during the intervention, by increasing level of complexity:

1. PREDICTION: What do you think it means?
2. What do you predict the colonists wanted? Peace or fighting?
3. When the king got the petition, do you think he read it?
4. How did the colonists feel when the king refused to read the petition?
5. What do you predict would happen to the colonists?
6. Do you think the colonists read Common Sense?
7. How did the king feel when he read it?
8. What do you predict Thomas Jefferson wrote as the reason for America's independence?

9. What did the king do when he got the Declaration of Independence?
10. What will happen next in history?

The time line was an extremely useful visual prompt. It helped the students understand the concept of what had happened and what would happen next. Since everything in the unit had happened in the past, having a visual to indicate which point in the past they were discussing was important in general, and specifically to teaching prediction. One thing that the teacher thought may have initially confused the students somewhat was the fact that prediction, especially in relation to its sign "PREDICTION", created an association with the future, and yet the teacher was asking them to predict a future of something that had happened in the past. Having a time line to indicate the "time period" for which the teacher was asking them to make predictions seemed to alleviate some of that confusion for the students.

For example, on the seventh day of the unit, after reviewing all the information the students had learned so far, the teacher pointed to the blank area on the time line and asked, "What happens next? What happens in this part?" One student predicted, "The king will read the book [referring to Common Sense] and be upset, because the book says no more control." This was a great prediction because it clearly showed that this student remembered what had been talked about the previous week. However, another student seemed somewhat confused at first about what to do. His first response was a retelling of the Boston Massacre, his favorite event. The teacher redirected him to the time line, went through each event, and, after each event, including the Boston Massacre, signed "FINISHED". Then the teacher pointed at the empty space on the time line and said, "What do you predict will happen here?" The lightbulb went off and he predicted, "Thomas Jefferson will write a paper and give it to Benjamin Franklin and George Washington." After being taught the meaning of prediction repetitively in a constructivist manner within multiple contexts, the students successfully grasped the meaning/concept. The meaning of prediction was reinforced in science and nonacademic situations, as previously indicated, and most important, its application was emphasized during reading tasks.

For example, on the first day of the teaching unit, right after the meaning of prediction was discussed in class, the students got an opportunity to make a prediction about whether the dinosaur in *How Do Dinosaurs Play with Their Friends?* would share his toys. The students were initially puzzled by the question, so the teacher re-read the first half of the story to help them recall what it was about. The teacher then modeled making a prediction for the students and said, "I predict the dinosaur will be selfish and won't share." The teacher wrote the prediction on the board. The teacher purposefully predicted incorrectly so that students would see that it was OK if a prediction was incorrect. What was important was that the students try to think about what was possible and make a prediction from that. Once the students saw the model, they understood what they were supposed to do and offered their predictions. As each students made his or her prediction, the teacher wrote it on the board. Two students predicted that the dinosaur would share, and the other two said the dinosaur would not share.

The teacher then asked, "How do we find out if our predictions are right or wrong?" This was an important question to ask and it was asked many times. It improved the students' metacognitive skills by reinforcing the idea of being an active reader and thinking about what might happen next in a story. After finishing the story, the teacher asked the students what happened. They replied, "SHARED". So, the teacher had them review each prediction and determine if the person who had made it was right or wrong. When asked, "Some predictions were wrong, is that OK?" the students quickly responded, "YES [because] TRIED". The lesson was then concluded with another review of what prediction meant.

Although the students initially struggled with comparing situations in their own lives to ones in the historical events, such comparisons became the information they remembered the best and became something they were more comfortable predicting later in the study. Discussing emotions and people's reactions to different events helped make history a story with cause-and-effect relationships, as well as making it more interesting to the students. An example of this occurred on day four of the intervention, when students were struggling to predict how the colonists felt after learning that the king had refused to read the Olive Branch Petition. By comparing the colonists' reaction to how they would feel if their teacher refused to read their homework and instead threw it in the garbage, all of the students were able to confidently predict and determine that the colonists would be upset or angry.

At the beginning of the intervention, none of the students understood the meaning of prediction; nevertheless, by the end of the two-and-a-half-week intervention, all of the students showed that they had acquired the concept by correctly answering the prediction questions. For instance, all of the participants provided acceptable answers to the final question on the social studies unit test, which required them to predict what would happen next in history and what the next unit would be about: "The King would fight the colonial army and that the colonists would win"; "The King would be in trouble with the colonial army"; "The colonists and George Washington would fight the King and his soldiers"; "George Washington would fight the British soldiers"; "George Washington would get mad, and he would ride on his horse and kill and fight the British troops."

Finally, although the students did attain some level of predicting ability, they still struggled in explaining the reasoning behind their predictions.

References

Brigham, M., & Hartman, M. C. (2010). What is your prediction? Teaching the metacognitive skill of prediction to a class of sixth- and seventh-grade students who are deaf. *American Annals of the Deaf, 155*(2), 137–143. https://www.jstor.org/stable/26235044

Desoete, A. (2009). Metacognitive prediction and evaluation skills and mathematical learning in third-grade students. *Educational Research and Evaluation, 15*(5), 435–446. doi: 10.1080/13803610903444485

Furnes, B., & Norman, E. (2015). Metacognition and reading: Comparing three forms of metacognition in normally developing readers and readers with dyslexia. *Dyslexia*, *21*, 273–284. doi: 10.1002/dys.1501

Garrett, A. J., Mazzocco, M. M. M., & Baker, L. (2006). Development of the metacognitive skills of prediction and evaluation in children with or without math disability. *Learning Disability Research and Practice*, *21*(2), 77–88. doi: 10.1111/j.1540-5826.2006.00208.x

Nolan, T. E. (1991). Self-questioning and prediction: Combining metacognitive strategies. *Journal of Reading*, *35*(2), 132–138. https://www.jstor.org/stable/40033122

Soto, C., Gutiérrez de Blume, A. P., Jacovina, M., McNamara, D., Benson, N., & Riffo, B. (2019). Reading comprehension and metacognition: The importance of inferential skills. *Cogent Education*, *6*(1), 1565067. https://doi.org/10.1080/2331186X.2019.1565067

10

Visualization

Visualization is a reaction to a picture or other graphic which is an externalization of a concept or idea, bringing it more clearly into consciousness. Visualization can stimulate more abstract, symbolical thinking, helping children to construct meaning for themselves as well as share their ideas with others and across contexts. Visualization involves developing competency with spatial interpretations, orientations and relations.

Definition

Visualization is to form or recall mental images or pictures, to make visual or visible, with the intention of communication of a message. It involves the creation of real or unreal images in the mind's eye. It can include visual images, but also images of sound, movement, touch, taste and smell. Images can be two-dimensional (as in a picture) or three-dimensional (as in a model). They can be static (as in a still picture) or dynamic (as in moving pictures or animations). Visual imagery has been an effective way to communicate both abstract and concrete ideas since the dawn of humanity, including cave paintings and Egyptian hieroglyphs. Images tend to be easier than linear text to perceive and memorize.

Pictures can:

- Engage the mind.
- Bring something more clearly into consciousness.
- Focus attention.
- Assist with the formation of ideas.
- Be a visual representation of a thought and/or idea.
- Allow ideas to be re-contextualized, revisited and revised.
- Mediate between a child's spontaneous concept and a child's scientific concept and move them to higher levels of thinking.
- Support visualizations that bridge the gap between perception-bound thinking and more abstract, symbolical thinking.
- Produce visual representations of ideas that allow children to work at a metacognitive level.
- Support the meta-visual capabilities that have been identified as critical to scientific understanding.
- Produce an external representation of a thought or idea so that it is then possible to interact with the idea both at an interpersonal and intrapersonal level.

Background

In 2005 Gilbert produced a whole edited book on visualization in science education, followed by another in 2008, but these were mainly focused on higher education (Gilbert, 2005; Gilbert et al., 2008). Höffler and Leutner (2007) produced a meta-analysis of studies on visual learning from dynamic vs. static materials across domains. However, of 26 selected studies, in only seven studies (27%) were the participants school students. The analysis yielded 76 comparisons of dynamic and static visualizations and a medium-sized overall advantage of instructional animations over static pictures (effect size 0.37). There were even more substantial effect sizes when the animation was representational rather than decorational (ES = 0.40), when the animation was highly realistic, e.g., video-based (ES = 0.76), and/or when procedural-motor knowledge was to be acquired (ES = 1.06).

This was followed up by McElhaney et al. (2015), who reviewed research to clarify the impacts of dynamic visualizations and identify instructional scaffolds that mediated their success. Dynamic visualizations for science were defined as computer-based, animated representations of scientific phenomena. Dynamic visualization technologies range from simple formats such as animated images or animated presentation slides to more complex modeling environments such as NetLOGO (http://ccl.northwestern.edu/net logo), Molecular Workbench (http://mw.concord.org) and PhET (http://phet.colorado.edu).

Meta-analysis synthesized 47 independent comparisons between dynamic and static materials and 76 comparisons that tested the effect of specific instructional scaffolds. A mean effect size of 0.27 was found, somewhat similar to Höffler and Leutner's (2007) result. Interestingly, studies in elementary/secondary schools (n = 10) gave an effect size of 0.27, while those in college and university environments (n = 37) only had an effect size of 0.07. There was a significant positive mean effect for inference outcomes (ES = 0.16), illustrating that dynamic visualizations appear to offer an advantage for conceptual learning. There were also significant effects in favor of long instructional durations (ES 0.33 vs. 0.06 for short) and classroom rather than laboratory studies (ES 0.28 vs. 0.06).

It was noted that much of the research on design of dynamic visualizations came from short laboratory studies of a single concept, rather than from classroom studies of complex phenomena. In addition, studies often conflated different types of visual material such as simulations, virtual laboratories and other multimedia instruction. Some studies that endorsed dynamic visualizations, such as pre-test–post-test designs or comparisons between dynamic visualizations and typical instruction, lacked controls for instructional design features unique to dynamic visualizations.

Learners could have difficulties with dynamic compared to static materials. First, learners with poor visual processing ability may struggle to understand dynamic visualizations. Second, dynamic visualizations may cognitively overload students with both the amount and complexity of information they depict, particularly if multiple representations are needed. Third, sequences of static images may require learners to actively integrate information and generate mental models, while dynamic visualizations may short-circuit this process. Fourth, dynamic visualizations of complex processes may give learners the illusion of understanding, discouraging them from seeking to repair gaps in their knowledge. That is, dynamic visualizations might be "deceptively clear" to learners in ways that static visuals were not.

Turning to individual papers, Cifuentes and Hsieh (2004) conducted a mixed-methods study on the effects of student-generated visualization on middle-schoolers' science concept learning. Students who visualized during study time were compared with those who did not. Visualization as a study strategy led to significantly improved test performances.

Following this up, Hsieh and Cifuentes (2006) explored the effects of student-generated visualization on paper and on computers as a study strategy for middle school science concept learning. Participants were eighth graders (n = 92) in six science classes at a junior high school. Two classes were randomly assigned to be the control group (n = 28), two classes to be the visualization/paper group (n = 30) and two classes to be the visualization/computer group (n = 34). In the visualization/paper group, students attended a four-session visualization workshop lasting 25 minutes per day. On days one, two, three and four, students were instructed in how to identify each of the three types of structures (cause-effect, sequence and comparison-contrast) and in how to use visual conventions (fishbone diagram, flowchart, matrix/table) to represent these structures on paper.

In a post-test-only-control-group design, the paper group and the computer group performed significantly better on the post-test than the control group. There was a large effect size (1.51) for the pairwise comparison of those participants who received the paper-form visualization workshop and constructed visualization on paper during study time compared to those participants who did not receive visualization workshop training and applied the unguided study strategy during study time. Additionally, the effect size for those students who received computer-based visualization workshop training and visualized on computers during study time compared to those participants who received non-visualization workshop training and applied the unguided study strategy while studying was 1.20 (large). However, no significant difference existed between the paper group and the computer group's scores.

Höffler et al. (2010) examined the role of visual cognitive style in two multimedia-based learning environments (text plus static pictures/animations). Highly developed visualizers (HDV) who learned with static pictures performed significantly better than HDV who learned with animations, and less developed visualizers (LDV) performed the same with static pictures or animations. For factual knowledge, there was a main effect in favor of HDV.

Chemistry high school students (n = 249) at one school completed the chemical reactions unit after covering chemical reactions concepts in textbook-centered activities (Chiu and Linn, 2012). Students were randomly assigned to external feedback and self-evaluation conditions. In the external feedback condition, students answered a multiple-choice question designed to test a main idea of the visualization. If the students correctly answered the question, they were told their answer was correct and were provided with a short explanation of the correct answer. Students then moved to the next step where they explained their understanding. If the students incorrectly answered the question, they were told their answer was incorrect and forced to revisit the visualization and follow instructions on how to interact with the visualization. Students could not access later steps in the unit until they correctly answered the question. This external feedback treatment occurred twice after two visualization steps. In the self-evaluation condition, students encountered the same question and were encouraged to revisit the visualization if they did not understand the answer. This group had no feedback but could access any step they wanted. In both groups, after either the feedback step or the self-evaluation step, students assessed and explained their understanding.

This study considered two assessments: one immediately after the second greenhouse visualization about how carbon dioxide impacts the global climate, and one about how excess reactants relate to balanced equations. Navigation logs of students progressing through the entire curriculum were used. Analysis of these logs focused on describing when students chose to revisit steps out of sequence, when students chose to revisit visualization steps and when students chose to revise answers to explanations. These measures were included as first indicators as to how students monitored their understanding while using the unit.

Overall, both groups showed significant gains from pre-test to post-test after controlling for pre-test score. These findings show that visualizations can be deceptively clear. A visualization can be so memorable that students become convinced they understand when they can recall only superficial features of what they have seen. To enhance student learning with visualizations, students must carefully observe and analyze what they see. Students observing a visualization of an explosion that at first glance depicts slow molecules that bounce around and suddenly speed up may think they understand. More careful analysis reveals that the reaction starts when one of the reactants spontaneously dissociates. The resultant free radicals attack the other reactant, releasing energy that causes additional dissociations and reactions. By experimenting with different dissociation and activation energies students could gain a deep understanding of chemical reactions. Emphasis on supports for self-monitoring can overcome this deceptive clarity. This finding resonates with work demonstrating an illusion of explanatory understanding and this illusion may be especially salient for learners using dynamic visualizations. People overestimate their explanatory knowledge as well as their ability to detect changes in visually presented information.

Specimen Program

"Visual literacy" can be defined as an ability enabling people to use visual images accurately and to behave appropriately in response. A visually literate person can: (1) interpret, understand and appreciate the meaning of visual messages; (2) communicate more effectively by applying the basic principles and concepts of visual design; (3) produce visual messages using computers and other technologies; and (4) use visual thinking to conceptualize solutions to problems. Visualizations provide means for making visible phenomena that are too small, large, fast or slow to see with the unaided eye. In addition, they illustrate invisible or abstract phenomena that cannot be observed or experienced directly.

Spatial ability may be defined as the ability to generate, retain, retrieve and transform well-structured visual images. There are several spatial abilities, each emphasizing different aspects of the process of image generation, storage, retrieval and transformation. Spatial ability involves representing, rotating and inverting objects in three dimensions when they are presented in two dimensions. Thus, visualization skills vary according to different levels of difficulty: (1) "Spatial visualization" is the ability to understand accurately three-dimensional (3D) objects from their two-dimensional (2D) representation; (2) "Spatial orientation" is the ability to imagine what a representation will look like from a different perspective; and (3) "Spatial relations" is the ability to visualize the effects of operations such as rotation, reflection and inversion, or to mentally manipulate objects.

Human cognitive architecture includes working memory of limited capacity and duration with partially separate visual and auditory channels, and an effective infinite long-term memory holding many schemas that can vary in their degree of automation. These cognitive structures have evolved to handle information that varies in the extent to which elements can be processed successively in working memory or, because they interact, must be processed simultaneously, imposing a heavy load on working memory. Cognitive load theory uses this combination of information and cognitive structures to guide instructional design.

There are three types of cognitive load: intrinsic, extraneous and germane. Intrinsic cognitive load occurs during the interaction between the nature of the material being learned and the expertise of the learner. Extraneous cognitive load is caused by factors that are not central to the material to be learned, such as presentation methods or activities that split attention between multiple sources of information, and these should be minimized as much as possible. Germane cognitive load enhances learning and results in task resources being devoted to schema acquisition and automation. Intrinsic cognitive load cannot be manipulated, in contrast to extraneous and germane cognitive load. Intrinsic, extraneous and germane cognitive load together cannot exceed working memory resources if learning is to occur.

Pictures have a superior effect on recall of information. The picture's superiority in explicit memory tasks is due to its stronger associative perceptual information than that of words. Pictures enable the extraction and retention of information that readers do not otherwise encode effectively. Pictures highlighting details effectively increase the recall of those details and pictures depicting relationships effectively increase recall of relational information. Secondary school students achieved the best results when using photographs of 3D molecular models or computer-generated models, while primary school students scored better when using concrete 3D models.

A sample of students was selected randomly from various schools in Greece by Korakakis et al. (2009) (63 in the first sample, 71 in the second and 78 in the third, 212 in total). In every classroom there were students of different intellectual ability, gender and economic status. The study aimed to determine whether the use of specific types of visualization (3D illustration, 3D animation and interactive 3D animation), combined with narration and text, contributed to the learning processes of eighth grade (13- and 14-year-old) students in science courses. The study used three different versions of an interactive multimedia application, each differing from the other two in a type of visuals. All the rest of the application components (narration, text, navigation, auxiliary tools, interface, etc.) were common to all three versions.

Seated at separate computers, each student worked with one version of the multimedia application during one school hour. The results indicated that multimedia applications with 3D animations and with interactive 3D animations increased the interest of students and made the material more appealing to them.

The most obvious and essential benefit of static visuals was that they left the time control of learning to the students and decreased the cognitive load.

Implementation

The multimedia application was created from scratch. The steps followed were: the drawing and production of all static 3D illustrations, the creation of 3D animations, and interactive 3D animations with the appropriate programming, the elaboration of the text and sound speech and the careful connection of all of the above elements in the final form of the multimedia application. The application explains in detail all the methods of separation which are presented in the current chemistry school book for eighth-grade students in Greece. The application included the following thematic units: distillation, fractional distillation, pouring, centrifugation, filtering, evaporation, paper chromatography, sieving and magnetic separation.

Four auxiliary windows were presented: the navigator bar, the window text (which was displayed whenever the user wished to read it), the window "instruments" and the window "useful". These windows were floating, as they could be moved to any part of the screen. The window menu, which was presented when the button "menu" was pressed on the navigator bar, consisted of the collapsible sub-menus: "file", "units", "finding", "exercises", "bibliography" and "authors". In the collapsible sub-menu "units", the user could return to any individual unit of the application. Also, in the collapsible sub-menu "finding", the user could find any experimental appliance that existed in the application. The 3D animations and interactive 3D animations had an operation of "repetition, pause, play", which made the comprehension of the phenomenon or the concept that they described easier. In addition, the interactive 3D animations featured the operation of free rotation with the mouse.

In the last part of the application, students were called to answer questions of various types. A total of nine questions were divided into three groups. The first group included multiple-choice questions, the second group of questions involved completion of blanks, while in the third group the questions were visualized. The percentage of correct answers was recorded and presented at the end of the application. The questions in all three versions were precisely the same and were presented in the same way. Also, in every question the student had the opportunity to check whether he/she had given a correct or a wrong answer. In the case of a wrong answer, the student had the chance to try once more, after which the question was locked.

During the execution of the application three files were stored on the computer's hard disk. In the first file the results of the evaluation test were registered. In the second file, the time that each user spent in each screen of the multimedia application as well as the number of visits in the same scene were registered. Similarly, in the third file the time that each user needed to answer each question was recorded. These three files were stored as text files then imported into an Excel spreadsheet. From the files the following information could be extracted: the percentage of correct answers per student; the questions answered correctly by each student; the time each student used to answer each question; the total time each student had dedicated in the question part of the application; the number of times each student had visited each question; the time that each student had dedicated in each scene of the application; the number of times each student had visited each scene; the total time each student had dedicated in the scenes of the application, apart from those with questions; the number of different scenes that each student had visited; and the number of questions that each student had checked.

In all three versions of the multimedia application, it was observed that the students allocated a lot more time to the first scene in comparison to the remaining scenes. Obviously, at the start the students needed time in order to examine closely the tools that were presented to them for use in each of the remaining scenes. That is, they tried to become familiar with the way of handling them, as well as to observe and comprehend the overall possibilities of the application. More than just a few students were hesitant and afraid to use the computer. Additional motivation was essential, even though directions on the use of the multimedia application had been given to them. At that point, students had the possibility of asking questions with regard to the use of the application. So, in an interactive multimedia application, the first main scene should not contain essential knowledge for the student, because the learning process is not yet effective.

In the version with interactive 3D animations, the students allocated more time to watching the scenes of the application (without the questions), compared to the one with static illustrations. It was observed that 3D animations and interactive 3D animations have a determined time duration and, in consequence, influence the time it takes to watch the scenes of a multimedia application. In contrast, the static illustrations do not determine the time. Thus, while in the first two versions the time was longer, in the third version it was shorter.

More time was also allocated by the students in order to comprehend animations, as compared to static illustrations. This was due to the fact that the application in the first two versions contained interactive controls (repetition, pause, play, and rotation in interactive 3D) and consequently the students made use of these possibilities. Many times, students not familiar with the application were unable to extract relative information from the dynamic visuals at the rate at which these were developing. This led the students to repeat the 3D animation or the interactive 3D animation, so that they had enough time to process these elements and interpret them. Nevertheless, because using the interactive controls can sometimes lead to the imposition of extraneous cognitive load, the addition of these elements is not always beneficial. Without suitable metacognitive ability, beginners are unable to effectively use such controls.

However, the first two versions of the application proved to be almost equivalent with regard to the number of scenes that the students watched. Also, the number of scenes watched decreased in the version with static illustrations (especially as time was passing). The results showed that the interest of students remained undiminished for the entire duration of watching the first two versions of the multimedia application, while in the third version the interest was limited, decreasing with time. Consequently, it could be concluded that multimedia applications with interactive 3D animation as well as 3D animation do indeed increase the interest of students and make such applications more attractive.

The most obvious benefits of static illustrations are summarized as follows: The static illustrations give students the time to control learning, decrease the cognitive load because each time students deal individually with an important step of learning, and encourage the relevant action as well as the effort to explain the changes from one frame to another. Also, the 3D models are used more by students of high spatial ability than by students of low spatial ability.

A positive relation was found between the time that students allocated to watching the multimedia application and the time that they used to answer the questions. Thus, as the time students allocated to the application was increased, the time to answer the questions was increased as well. A possible explanation is that students who studied the application thoroughly also studied the questions thoroughly before they answered them. Another possible explanation is that the students, who had some difficulty and hesitancy in using the computers, dedicated more time to the follow-up of the application and in the answering of questions.

It became apparent in the first two versions that as students allocated more time to watch the scenes, the percentage of correct answers decreased. It was found that there was a negative relation between the percentage of correct answers to the questions and the time that each student allocated to watching the multimedia application. The increased time of watching the scenes in these two versions was due to the fact that the students studied interactive 3D as well as 3D animations with the help of the interactive controls. The negative relation can be explained by the fact that the effect of the first two versions was to increase the cognitive load of the students. This wore out the students and reduced their learning capacity temporarily. In general, the increase of extraneous cognitive load during the presentation of a way of learning had as a consequence the reduction of effectiveness in the resolution of problems by the students.

The most important conclusion was that the contribution of all three types of visualization was differentiated. In particular, both interactive 3D animations and 3D animations dominated the 3D illustrations regarding increase of interest, while the latter are the least attractive to the students. On the other hand, the 3D illustrations dominated the first two regarding the reduction of cognitive load, as the interactive or dynamic 3D models may lead to cognitive overload problems, as multimedia environments are assumed to generate a heavy cognitive load.

References

Chiu, J. L., & Linn, M. C. (2012). The role of self-monitoring in learning chemistry with dynamic visualizations. In A. Zohar & Y. J. Dori (Eds.), *Metacognition in Science Education: Trends in Current Research*. London: Springer-Verlag. doi: 10.1007/978-94-007-2132-6_7

Cifuentes, L., & Hsieh, Y. C. J. (2004). Visualization for middle school students' engagement in science learning. *Journal of Computers in Mathematics and Science Teaching*, *23*(2), 109–137. https://www.learntechlib.org/primary/p/12874/

Gilbert, J. K. (Ed.) (2005). *Visualization in Science Education*. Dordrecht: Springer.

Gilbert, J. K., Reiner, M., & Nakhleh, M. (Eds.) (2008). *Visualization: Theory and Practice in Science Education*. Dordrecht: Springer.

Höffler, T. N., & Leutner, D. (2007). Instructional animation versus static pictures: A meta-analysis. *Learning and Instruction*, *17*, 722–738. https://doi.org/10.1016/j.learninstruc.2007.09.013

Höffler, T. N., Prechtl, H., & Nerdel, C. (2010). The influence of visual cognitive style when learning from instructional animations and static pictures. *Learning and Individual Differences*, *20*, 479–483. https://doi.org/10.1016/j.lindif.2010.03.001

Hsieh, Y. C. J., & Cifuentes, L. (2006). Student-generated visualization as a study strategy for science concept learning. *Educational Technology & Society*, *9*(3), 137–148. https://www.jstor.org/stable/10.2307/jeductechsoci.9.3.137

Korakakis, G., Pavlatou, E. A., Palyvos, J. A., & Spyrellis, N. (2009). 3D visualization types in multimedia applications for science learning: A case study for 8th grade students in Greece. *Computers & Education*, *52*, 390–401. doi: 10.1016/j.compedu.2008.09.011

McElhaney, K. W., Chang, H. Y., Chiu, J. L., & Linn, M. C. (2015). Evidence for effective uses of dynamic visualisations in science curriculum materials. *Studies in Science Education*, *51*(1), 49–85. doi: 10.1080/03057267.2014.984506

11

Diagrams

Diagrams are a particular kind of visualization (see Chapter 10), but have a rich literature of their own. "Diagrams" can include concept maps, mind maps, Vee diagrams, Venn diagrams, geographical maps, semantic webs, organizational charts, Gantt charts, SWOT diagrams, fishbone diagrams, Roundhouse diagrams, flowcharts, funnel charts, tree diagrams, line graphs, histograms, scatter plots, pie charts and frequency curves, to name but a few.

Definition

A diagram is a visual snapshot of information.

Background

Diagramming is a very common metacognitive strategy, used across planning, monitoring and evaluating. Increasingly, computers are used to support learners' production of graphics regardless of their level of artistic skill. An early paper by Novak (1990) describes two metacognitive tools (concept mapping and Vee diagramming) and reports on research using these tools from grade 1 through to university. The issues of the rote nature of much school learning and the resistance of students (and teachers) to move to meaningful learning strategies fostered by concept mapping and Vee diagramming were discussed. Even at this early date, a variety of qualitative and quantitative research studies strongly supported the value of these metacognitive tools for both cognitive and affective gains.

One of the visualization techniques commonly used by learners for knowledge construction is concept mapping. Concept mapping is *a diagram that depicts suggested relationships between concepts* so you can better understand and communicate their connections. As students construct concept maps, they actively revise and manipulate the information to be learned and look for meaningful concept connections. Concept mapping also enhances students' self-esteem through the sense of accomplishment of constructing a map and the subsequent realization that they can extract concepts to construct their own meaning.

Kinchin et al. (2000) describe three major patterns of concept maps: "spoke", "chain" and "net" structures. Spoke has a central node from which several spokes emerge. Chain is a line of concepts. Nets connect several concepts and offer more than one route between them. The patterns are interpreted as being indicators of progressive levels of understanding. Identification of these differences may help the classroom teacher to focus teaching for more effective learning and may be used as a basis for structuring groups in collaborative settings. This approach to analyzing concept maps is of value because it suggests teaching approaches that help students integrate new knowledge and build upon their existing naïve concepts.

A Roundhouse diagram is different entirely (Ward & Wandersee, 2002). It is a large circle divided into sections (typically seven), with a central small circle in which the conclusions from the seven sections can be put. The process by which Roundhouse diagramming helps learners bootstrap their current understandings to reach the intended meaningful understanding of complex science topics was elucidated in this study by Ward and Wandersee. The main findings were that: (a) it is crucial that relevant prior knowledge and dysfunctional alternative conceptions are not ignored during new learning if low-performing science students are to understand science well; (b) as the student's mastery of the Roundhouse diagram construction improved, so did science achievement; and (c) the student's apt choice of concept-related visual icons aided progress toward meaningful understanding of complex science concepts.

Cuevas et al. (2002) investigated how individual characteristics interacted with conceptual manipulations in a computer-based environment. Incorporating diagrams into the training facilitated performance on measures of integrative knowledge (i.e., the integration and application of task-relevant knowledge), but had no significant effect on measures of declarative knowledge (i.e., mastery of basic factual knowledge). Diagrams additionally facilitated the development of accurate mental models and significantly improved the instructional efficiency of the training (i.e., a higher level of performance was achieved with less mental effort). Finally, diagrams effectively scaffolded participants' metacognition, improving their meta-comprehension accuracy (i.e., their ability to accurately monitor their comprehension). These beneficial effects of diagrams on learners' cognitive and metacognitive processes were found to be strongest for participants with low verbal ability.

It has been argued that teaching high school students about the conventions of diagrams can improve diagrammatic reasoning (Miller et al., 2016). In a study of 59 eighth-grade (middle school) students from three classrooms, conventions of diagrams instruction using warm-ups on laptop computers was delivered, while control students received only warm-up questions. Students receiving conventions of diagrams warm-ups for ten weeks (but not four weeks) improved their diagrammatic reasoning more than control students. Treatment students' answers were more accurate than control students' answers, especially on easy questions. The discourse of pairs of students showed that treatment students talked about the diagrams more and made more inferences. Results suggested that conventions of diagrams instruction could be integrated into classroom routines using computer-delivered warm-ups and was helpful (if sustained) both for improving diagrammatic reasoning and for supporting learning science content.

Specimen Program

The effectiveness of using a Vee diagram to aid students in comprehending and learning science concepts meaningfully was studied by Alvarez and Risko (2007). The Vee diagram heuristic was developed to enable students to understand the structure of knowledge (e.g., relational networks, hierarchies, combinations) and to understand the process of knowledge construction. The assumption is that knowledge is not absolute, but rather it is dependent upon the concepts, theories and methodologies by which we view the world. To learn meaningfully, individuals must choose to relate new knowledge to relevant concepts and propositions they already know. The Vee diagram aids students in this linking process by acting as a metacognitive tool that requires students to make explicit connections between previously learned underlying conceptual aspects and newly acquired information.

    The Vee diagram separates theoretical/conceptual (thinking) on the left from the methodological (doing) elements of inquiry on the right. The two sides actively interact with each other through the use of the focus or telling question(s) that directly relates to events and/or objects. Knowledge elements are arrayed around the Vee diagram and represent units that form the structure of some segment or portion of knowledge required to construct a new meaning or piece of knowledge. A lesson using a Vee diagram is explained in which the teacher guides students in understanding the concept of "seed germination".

Implementation

The teacher was knowledgeable on the purpose, terminology and use of hierarchical concept maps and Vee diagrams. She used the following guidelines: (1) Before using the Vee, students should first be familiar with and be able to construct concept maps. Once students are acquainted with using concept maps, they are shown how concept maps supply most of the information on the "left side" of the Vee. This also familiarized students with two elements of the Vee: concepts and events and/or objects. (2) Explain and define the terms: (a) concepts, (b) events and objects, (c) records of events/objects (facts), and (d) focus question(s). Records are the facts that are gathered about events/objects being observed. Focus questions guide the kind of records students are to make. The kinds and types of records made are determined by the question(s) asked. Students are shown by demonstration and explanation how records are used to observe events or objects. Based on observations of events or objects, records are made (e.g., field notes, interviews, measurements of time, length, weight, height, temperature, audio and videotapes, documents and so forth).

(3) After the records have been made of the facts, the information is transformed into a format that allows the student to construct answers to the focus question. This information is organized and put into a format (such as a table, graph, chart, diagram and so forth). (4) Using the information from the transformed data, knowledge claims are constructed to answer the focus question(s). Students' thoughts are gathered as to the accordance of these claims with their prior knowledge about the concepts and principles already known to them. (5) Principles and theories follow knowledge claims. Principles tell how events or objects appear to behave. For example, in the experiment with sprouting seeds, a principle derived from the outcome is "Plants need air, water, soil and light to grow." Theories show why events or objects appear to behave as they do. (6) Value claims are statements of self-worth and are an expression of feelings about the findings of the inquiry.

In accordance with these guidelines, the teacher introduced examples of concept maps and Vee diagrams to her students. The teacher placed her 28 students into six groups to observe the participation of each student. She then had them construct hierarchical concept maps for the corresponding reading assignments for the unit. For example, students constructed a concept map on the topic of energy. One student approached this topic by showing that energy can be demonstrated by water, which he described as turning into snow, ice and liquid which are forms of matter that can be solids, liquids or gases. His concept map showed these hierarchical relationships with elaborations and examples.

Then a science experiment investigating "sprouting plants" under four conditions was conducted. All four conditions contained beans that had been soaked overnight in water and then were placed in a jar suspended between paper toweling and the inner glass. The four conditions were: (1) an inch of water at the bottom of the jar with wet paper toweling surrounding the inner portion of the jar that supported the beans against the jar with the top opened; (2) an inch of water at the bottom of the jar with wet paper toweling supporting the beans against the jar with a plastic covering so that air could not get in; (3) an inch of water at the bottom of the jar with paper toweling with the top opened, placed in a dark compartment without light; and (4) no water in the jar with dry paper toweling with the top opened.

The teacher then gave each student a skeletal Vee diagram that contained these headings: focus question, event/object, concepts to be investigated, records, transformations, knowledge claims, value claims, theory and principles. She used a questioning strategy to guide students' notations on their Vee diagram: (1) What is the telling question? What is it about? (2) What concepts are needed to ask the question? (3) What methods/procedures are useful in answering the question(s)? (4) What answers are produced? and (5) What value do these claims have?

The purpose of these questions was to guide the learner's inquiry of a topic under study by focusing attention to the components arrayed around the Vee. The teacher began by calling attention to the seeds that had been soaked in water overnight. She asked "What do you suppose will happen in each of these four conditions?" The intent of such questions was to elicit reflective thinking from the students by guiding them in formulating their focus question. The students were then asked to describe the four conditions and list those concepts that they believed were necessary to understand the target concept stated in the focus question. Twice daily, the students then individually recorded the time of day and what they observed was taking place in these four conditions in their journals.

Students were encouraged to share their records of these events and ask questions of each other within their group and with the teacher during their data collection. After six days of observations, each group was asked to use their recorded data to construct a graph depicting their daily observations. Each student was then asked to develop a hierarchical concept map showing the results of their findings. Upon completion, students within groups shared their maps with each other. Students were informed that they could revise and reconstruct their maps as a result of these comparisons and discussions.

Using the transformed information derived from their graph and concept maps, the students began generating answers to the focus question. These answers were listed under knowledge claims. From these knowledge claims, students constructed principles that hypothesized how the events occurred during the experiment. These principles led them to devise a theory that attempted to explain why the events they observed appeared to act as they did. Students made judgments as to the worth of these findings by listing them under value claims.

Individual Vee diagrams were scored on a quality point scale using the following criteria: focus question (0–3 points), objects/events (0–3), theory, principles and concepts (0–4), records/transformations (0–4), and knowledge claims (0–4), with a maximum score of 18. All students were able to complete the component parts of the Vee with success. Student interviews by the teacher indicated that the Vee diagrams helped them to understand what was taking place in the experiment. The students indicated that they found making charts of the records and hierarchical concept maps of the results of the experiment helpful in understanding the idea of "sprouting seeds".

The students became interested in the experiment and were able to discuss the knowledge claims in relation to their focus question and events. The Vee diagram provided an evaluation instrument to determine how well students understood their focus question and were able to relate the four conditions comprising the events to their findings. This, in turn, enabled the provision of differentiated feedback according to their understanding of concepts (e.g., sprout, germinate), theory, principles, records, knowledge and value claims.

As a metacognitive tool the Vee diagram aided students in monitoring the concepts, events and facts needed to answer their focus question concerning "germination". These elements, combined with the other components arrayed on the Vee, were revisited by these students during this experiment and enabled them to search their prior knowledge of the targeted concept under study and extend this knowledge through the formulation of graphs, hierarchical concept maps, knowledge and value claims, and by linking principles to a plausible theory. Conceptual understanding of the science concept was also enhanced by conversations emanating from other group members and the teacher as the experiment progressed.

References

Alvarez, M. C., & Risko, V. J. (2007). *The use of Vee diagrams with third graders as a metacognitive tool for learning science concepts*. Tennessee State University, Teaching and Learning Faculty Research. Paper 5. http://digitalscholarship.tnstate.edu/teaching/5

Cuevas, H. M., Fiore, S. M., & Oser, R. L. (2002). Scaffolding cognitive and metacognitive processes in low verbal ability learners: Use of diagrams in computer-based training environments. *Instructional Science*, *30*, 433–464. https://doi.org/10.1023/A:1020516301541

Kinchin, I. M., Hay, D. B., & Adams, A. (2000). How a qualitative approach to concept map analysis can be used to aid learning by illustrating patterns of conceptual development. *Educational Research*, *42*(1), 43–57. doi: 10.1080/001318800363908

Miller, B. W., Cromley, J. G., & Newcombe, N. S. (2016). Improving diagrammatic reasoning in middle school science using conventions of diagrams instruction. *Journal of Computer Assisted Learning*, *32*, 374–390. doi: 10.1111/jcal.12143

Novak, J. D. (1990). Concept maps and Vee diagrams: Two metacognitive tools to facilitate meaningful learning. *Instructional Science*, *19*, 29–52. https://doi.org/10.1007/BF00377984

Ward, R. E., & Wandersee, J. H. (2002). Struggling to understand abstract science topics: A Roundhouse diagram-based study. *International Journal of Science Education*, *24*(6), 575–591. https://doi.org/10.1080/09500690110074017

12

Mnemonics

Mnemonic training has been shown to be an effective memory aid. It has been hypothesized to work because it reduces and organizes the material to be learned, provides more than one access route to memory storage which increases the probability of successful retrieval, and heightens the level of information processing regarding association.

Definition

A mnemonic (pronounced ni-mon-ik) is a device that helps you learn and remember more complex information by associating what is to be learned with a pattern of letters, acronyms, acrostics, numbers, special rhymes and poems, images or songs.

The most common types of mnemonic devices are acronyms and acrostics, association, chunking, the method of loci and songs and rhymes. Of these, acronyms and acrostics are probably the most familiar type. *Acronyms* use a letter to represent each word or phrase or concept that needs to be remembered. An *acrostic* is similar except that instead of relating to a word, it relates to a sentence. However, people learn in different ways and mnemonics that work for one person may not be helpful for another.

Examples of mnemonics include:

The eight planets in order in the solar system – Mercury, Venus, Earth, Mars, Jupiter, Saturn, Uranus, Neptune – can be remembered with: My Very Educated Mother Just Served Us Noodles.
ROY G BIV is an acronym to remember the order of the colors in a rainbow: red, orange, yellow, green, blue, indigo and violet.
"i before e except after c" is a rhyme to help remember a spelling convention in English relating to the order of letters in words.

Mnemonic systems work because: (1) the capacity of short-term memory is limited, so small basic units of input enhance memorization; (2) internal organization such as categories or chunks are needed due to difficulty in learning ordered relationships; (3) well-incorporated associations aid memory search during retrieval; and (4) depth of processing is enhanced, i.e., users are given a means to access complex information too hard to recall.

Much of the research literature is in higher education, but some is in schools and mnemonic training has been demonstrated to facilitate the memory of individuals with learning difficulties. Visual imagery and verbal elaboration are effective, but visual imagery might be more effective, especially with the less able student. The use of explicit feedback, highly familiar stimuli and paced task presentation also enhance effectiveness. Teacher-provided mnemonics are generally superior to self-generated ones – this is unsurprising as generating mnemonics takes considerable mental effort. Students with learning difficulty can remember mnemonic devices, but have problems transferring this to dissimilar tasks, i.e., generalization is difficult. Recommendations to foster generalization include intensive training and explicit feedback.

Background

There is a systematic review of the effects of mnemonic interventions on academic outcomes for youth with disabilities

(Wolgemuth et al., 2008), but it only focused on students with disabilities and only on secondary age pupils. Previous studies of this kind had reported an overall effect size of 1.62 (very large) and mnemonic strategies were successful for special needs students in mathematics, science and vocabulary instruction. Overall, 2800 studies were reduced to 20 studies intervening with 669 young people with learning disabilities. The mean effect size was 1.38 (very large). The findings strongly supported the efficacy of mnemonic interventions across study methods, educational settings, student ages and disabilities in the improvement of academic performance, typically measured by recall of word meanings or factual information.

Turning to individual studies, in a study of students with learning disabilities in a middle school, Mastropieri et al. (1997) taught the chronological order of 32 U.S. presidents over a six-week period. For three weeks, they were taught using a modified mnemonic keyword strategy. For the next three weeks, they were taught using rehearsal and representational pictures. After a further two weeks, students were given a delayed post-test. They were asked to provide the numerical order of the president given a president name; and the president's name given the numerical order. Results revealed a significant main effect for the instructional condition.

Hsu (1999) investigated the effects of a combination of a mnemonic-imagery strategy and a metacognitive-questioning strategy upon students' long-term retention of complex factual information and transfer of the trained strategy to new learning in history. Five groups including 213 eighth-grade students were randomly assigned to five treatment conditions: mnemonic picture only, mnemonic picture plus metacognitive questioning, imagery-generating only, imagery-generating plus metacognitive questioning, and no strategy instruction. Seven Chinese history lessons were taught by a single teacher to the five groups, with the last two lessons used to measure retention and learning strategy transfer. Comparisons between the different treatments yielded a significant main effect for metacognitive questioning on the retention measure and a significant main effect for imagery on the transfer measure. Trained students overwhelmingly showed more satisfaction with the new approach than with traditional approaches in terms of effectiveness, interest level and motivation.

High school students with learning disabilities were investigated by Whitescarver (2018), who explored the effectiveness of mnemonic devices on the acquisition and retention of social studies vocabulary. Six students participated. During baseline, students were evaluated on their acquisition of vocabulary taught using traditional methods. During intervention, students were evaluated on their retention of vocabulary taught using teacher-created mnemonic devices. Results showed that the use of mnemonic devices increased the acquisition and retention of vocabulary. Furthermore, a student survey showed satisfactory ratings in ease and enjoyment of using mnemonics.

Roebers et al. (2019) studied cue utilization in elementary school. Cue utilization quantifies the degree to which an individual uses mnemonic experiences during task mastery to inform monitoring processes. Cue utilization fluency was assessed by recording children's response times in a recognition test and relating these to confidence ratings. A sample of second and fourth graders was assessed three times over one year in terms of their recognition performance, the time needed to select an alternative and their monitoring accuracy. Results revealed age differences in monitoring accuracy, cue utilization and cue validity. While monitoring accuracy increased over time in both age groups, cue utilization increased only in the younger children.

Specimen Program

Paige (1981) conducted a study with 18 students with learning difficulties, mean chronological age 15 and mean IQ 68. The aim was to determine if the combination of mnemonic and metacognitive training would lead to the transfer of mnemonic techniques in such children. The participants were trained to use a mnemonic strategy on a paired associate list and the transfer measures included multiple associate and free recall lists. The dependent measures included study times and recall accuracy.

The treatment group receiving mnemonic and metacognitive training was expected to exhibit superior memory transfer in comparison to the control group, which received no training. Furthermore, the treatment group was also expected to utilize longer study times than the control group and to utilize the trained strategy for all tasks (while the control group would not use the strategy spontaneously).

Implementation

The stimulus and response items of each of the paired associate and multiple associate lists, and the items of the free recall list, consisted of common and easily identified pictures of concrete nouns. The 100 pictures were extracted from the Peabody Picture Vocabulary Test. Cards illustrated two examples of paired associate trials, used for training purposes.

Each picture was categorized (e.g., animals, clothing, food, etc.) and the following restrictions applied: pictures from the same category were not used to form a pair or triplet, obvious relationships were avoided (e.g., bird/tree), and pairs and triplets were capable of being joined by a connective verb. Two ten-item paired associate lists were used for training. Two further ten-item paired associate lists were used for maintenance measures, two ten-item paired associate lists were used to measure near generalization, and two ten-item free recall lists were used to measure far generalization.

All participants were tested individually. They were told: "We're going to play a fun game. I'm going to show you one picture and you tell me what picture goes with it. The same two pictures always go together. Now I'll show you the first two pictures that go together and we'll see if you remember." For the first five pairs of paired associate list matches, the item pair was presented, then removed and the participant was asked to name what belonged with the stimulus item. After the participant responded, the card was exposed again to provide feedback. After the fifth pair, the participant was asked to recall all five remaining items in one block.

The second paired associate training list was then presented to all participants, who were asked to recall the response items after being exposed to the individually presented stimulus items. The treatment group received special instruction in mnemonics and metacognition, and was taught to visually imagine the paired associate pairs interacting, monitor their study efforts and verbalize the task requirements and procedures. The control group was instructed to verbalize similarly but received no further training.

Then maintenance testing proceeded, similar to what had gone before. The participants paced themselves and their study times and use of the strategy were recorded. Then the stimulus card for each pair was separately exposed and the participant asked "What goes with this?" Each response was recorded. Turning to near generalization, all participants were instructed "We're going to play some more, but this time I'm going to show you three pictures that always go together. Then I'll show you one picture and you tell me what two pictures come next."

For far generalization, all participants were told: "Now we are going to play a different game. I'll show you some pictures and when I have finished, I want you to tell me what they were." The free recall list was used for this procedure and participants paced their own exposure time, which was recorded.

In terms of training effects, the metacognition plus mnemonics treatment group recalled a significantly greater number of correct items on the paired associate task compared to the control group (effect size partial eta-squared = 0.31, large). They also recalled a greater number than the control group on the multiple associate task (effect size partial eta-squared = 0.30, large). However, on the free recall task, the difference was not significant.

In terms of study times, the metacognition plus mnemonics group studied for longer than controls on both tasks: paired associate (effect size partial eta-squared = 0.28, large) and multiple associate (effect size partial eta-squared = 0.30, large). Again, results for the free recall task were not significant. Turning to immediate vs. delayed test effects, there were no significant differences in any measures.

Strategy use was determined by overt verbalization while studying the task items. All verbalizations that contained the strategy, paraphrased the strategy or used critical components of the strategy, were regarded as use of the strategy. The use of the strategy was very different between the metacognition plus mnemonic group and the controls. None of the controls used it, while the experimental group certainly did. This difference was significant for the paired associate task (effect size partial eta-squared = 0.50, very large) and the multiple associate task (effect size partial eta-squared = 0.50, very large), but was not significant for the free recall task. Use of strategy remined constant across trials, i.e., if the strategy was used on the paired associate and multiple associate tasks on the immediate test, it was also used on the delayed test.

As the two groups were homogeneous at the outset, differences in performance could be attributed to the training, which affected performance. The experimental group recalled a significantly higher number of paired associate and multiple associate items than did the control group. However, training did not appear to affect performance on the free recall task. The experimental group also studied the items longer than controls, but neither group studied longer for the free recall task. The experimental group used the strategy while controls did not, but the experimental group tended to discard the strategy when it came to the free recall task. Thus, the combination of metacognitive training and mnemonics was very successful in the short term, but not in far generalization. However, Paige (1981) is to be commended for including the far generalization test.

References

Hsu, C. H. (1999). *The effects of a combination of a mnemonic imagery strategy and metacognitive questioning on learning factual information of history.* Ph.D. thesis, University of Texas at Austin. https://www.proquest.com/openview/89d5c9fe4b41cd0b7680a30f0635d792/1?pq-origsite=gscholar&cbl=18750&diss=y

Mastropieri, M. A., Scruggs, T. E., & Whedon, C. (1997). Using mnemonic strategies to teach information about U.S. presidents: A classroom-based investigation. *Learning Disability Quarterly*, *20*, 13–21. https://doi.org/10.2307/1511089

Paige, L. Z. (1981). *Teaching skill generalization: Metacognitive and mnemonic training of educable mentally retarded children*. Master's thesis, Fort Hays University Graduate School. 1825. doi: 10.58809/VNBZ4715. https://scholars.fhsu.edu/theses/1825

Roebers, C. M., Mayer, B., Steiner, M., Bayard, N. S., & van Loon, M. H. (2019). The role of children's metacognitive experiences for cue utilization and monitoring accuracy: A longitudinal study. *Developmental Psychology*, *55*(10), 2077–2089. https://doi.org/10.1037/dev0000776

Whitescarver, E. L. (2018). *Effect of mnemonics on the vocabulary acquisition and retention of high school students with learning disabilities*. M.A. thesis, Rowan University. https://rdw.rowan.edu/etd/2567

Wolgemuth, J. R., Cobb, R. B., & Alwell, M. (2008). The effects of mnemonic interventions on academic outcomes for youth with disabilities: A systematic review. *Learning Disabilities Research & Practice*, *23*(1), 1–10. https://doi.org/10.1111/j.1540-5826.2007.00258.x

13

Self-Assessment

The primary purposes of self-assessment are to boost student learning and achievement, as well as to promote self-regulation, or the tendency to monitor and manage one's own learning. Self-assessment is done on drafts of works in progress in order to inform revision and improvement; it is not a matter of having students determine their own grades. It is a key element in formative assessment because it involves students in thinking about the quality of their own work, rather than relying on their teacher as the sole source of evaluative judgments. As students self-assess, they must perforce reflect on the qualities of good and less good work, and consequently make efforts to improve – i.e., metacognition and self-regulation.

Metacognition in general and self-assessment in particular commonly occur before an act of production of work (forethought) (for instance when providing the students with assessment criteria, so that they are able to set realistic goals for the task), during that act (self-reflection), and after that act has concluded (since monitoring can be done with more accuracy, as there is a clearer understanding of the final learning outcome). One of the most direct pieces of empirical evidence for self-assessment having an effect on all phases comes from a study by Panadero and Romero (2014). In this study, the use of explicit assessment criteria was shown to have a significant impact on the forethought phase (partial eta-squared effect size = 0.26, very large), the performance phase (ES = 0.08, medium), and the self-reflection phase (ES = 0.22, very large). Thus, the preparatory/forethought phase of learning strategy was affected the most.

Definition

Self-assessment is monitoring one's own learning processes and products to make judgments of merit or worth about one's outcomes. Learners identify standards and/or criteria applying to their work and make judgments about the extent to which they have met those criteria and standards. Subsequently adjustments are made that deepen learning and enhance performance. Clear assessment criteria are crucial, and these may be developed with students in discussion or simply inflicted upon them (the latter option yielding worse results).

Background

There are several reviews and meta-analyses of self-assessment. For example, Brown and Harris (2013) reviewed 23 K-12 studies, including a wide variety of operationalizations of self-assessment. The median effect was between 0.40 and 0.45. The authors also noted that self-assessment seemed to improve student performance across a range of grade levels and subject areas, but that it seemed to be the implementation of the intervention, rather than its type, which generated positive effects.

In a meta-analysis by Sitzmann et al. (2010), the correlation between self-assessment and learning was stronger for courses that included feedback (ES = 0.28) than for courses that did not include feedback (ES = 0.14). Furthermore, when students self-assessed without receiving feedback on their accuracy, the relationship with learning was weaker (0.29) compared to situations where students received external feedback (ES = 0.51).

More recently, Panadero et al. (2017) meta-analyzed the effects of self-assessment on students' self-regulated learning and self-efficacy. A total of 19 studies were included in the four different meta-analyses conducted. However, studies involving students from elementary school were few (two), while studies from secondary school and higher education were more evenly represented (ten and eight studies respectively). The effect sizes from the three meta-analyses on different measures of self-regulated learning (SRL) were 0.23 (Learning SRL), 0.65 (Negative SRL), and 0.43 (Qualitative SRL). The effect size on self-efficacy was 0.73. Gender was a significant moderator, with girls benefiting more. Certain self-assessment components (such as self-monitoring) were significant moderators of self-efficacy.

Turning to individual studies, Kaderavek et al. (2004) examined aspects of self-assessment and oral narrative production in 401 children between 5 and 12 years of age. Oral narrative production was evaluated through the Test of Narrative Language. Self-assessment of narrative performance was determined by asking children to self-evaluate their ability to "tell a good story" by pointing to one of five pictures from a "very happy face" (rated 5) to a "very sad face" (rated 1). Older children (≥ 10 years of age) were more accurate than younger children in their ability to self-evaluate narrative performance; there was a significant difference in narrative production skills between children who rated themselves as poor performers (self-rating of 1 or 2) and children who were high self-raters (≥ 3); narrative self-evaluation varied in relation to gender, with males more frequently overestimating their narrative ability; and children with poor narrative ability were more likely to overestimate the quality of their narrative production than were good narrators.

Jacobson and Viko (2010) investigated the chemistry achievement over eight weeks of those exposed to self-assessment strategies and those not exposed, with an interest in any gender differences. Participants were 192 10-year-old students (91 boys, 101 girls). Instruments used were the Chemistry Achievement Test, Self-Assessment Scale and Chemistry Self-efficacy Scale (CSS). The pre-post mean gain on self-assessment skills was 3.00 and 0.31 for controls. On chemistry achievement, the pre-post mean gain was 28.57 and 8.62 for controls. On self-efficacy, the pre-post mean gain was 24.88 and -0.57 for controls. There was no difference between males and females on any measure.

Think-aloud and self-assessment strategies in chemistry were compared by Dike et al. (2017) in relation to controls. The think-aloud group was 140 students, the self-assessment group 120 students, and controls 100 students (total 360), drawn from three secondary schools. The instrument for data collection was a 25-item multiple-choice chemistry achievement test. Students taught with think-aloud metacognitive strategies performed better than self-assessment students, who in turn were better than controls. Either think-aloud or self-assessment was effective and both should be utilized by teachers.

Kusuma and Zaenuri (2019) aimed to investigate creative problem solving with recitation and self-assessment in grade 7. Observation, tests and interviews were employed. The creative problem-solving learning model with recitation and self-assessment showed good quality in planning, the learning process and the final result of learning. Subjects with low metacognition ability were able to fulfill the fluency indicator, but not the flexibility, novelty or elaboration indicators. Participants with moderate metacognition ability were able to fulfill the fluency and elaboration indicators but not the flexibility and novelty indicators. Subjects with high metacognition ability fulfilled all indicators.

Specimen Program

Arguably, in order for effective self-assessment to occur, students need: awareness of the value of self-assessment, access to clear criteria on which to base the assessment, a specific task or performance to assess, models of self-assessment, direct instruction in and assistance with self-assessment, practice, cues regarding when it is appropriate to self-assess, and opportunities to revise and improve the task or performance. Rubrics may well help with self-assessment. A rubric is usually a one- or two-page document that lists self-assessment criteria and describes varying levels of quality, from excellent to poor, for a specific assignment.

Our specimen program is set in the context of artificial intelligence (Roll et al., 2011), particularly the Self-Assessment Tutor, an intelligent tutoring system for improving the accuracy of the judgments students make regarding their own knowledge. A classroom evaluation of the Self-Assessment Tutor with 84 students found that they improved their ability to identify their strengths. In addition, students transferred their improved self-assessment skills to corresponding sections in the Geometry Cognitive Tutor. However, students often failed to identify their knowledge deficits and failed to update their assessments following unsuccessful solution attempts.

Specifically, the study addressed the following questions: (1) Do students who lack domain knowledge also make less accurate self-assessments? (2) How do students use their actual problem-solving ability to calibrate their self-assessments? (3) Does the Self-Assessment Tutor help students improve the accuracy of their self-assessments? (4) Do improved self-assessment skills transfer to unsupported sections of the problem-solving environment?

Implementation

The goals of the Self-Assessment Tutor are to help students get in the habit of assessing their ability, improve the accuracy of their self-assessments and use their self-assessments to inform strategy choice. The Self-Assessment Tutor, an intelligent tutoring system, adheres to several principles of metacognitive tutoring. It is a learning by doing environment in that students learn to self assess by practicing self-assessment in the context of mathematical problem solving. The Self-Assessment Tutor helps students set the following subgoals: predict one's own ability, attempt to solve the problem, reflect on the experience, and plan future interaction. Since students who identify their own errors learn better than students who receive feedback on their errors, the Self-Assessment Tutor helps students to identify their self-assessment errors. Adaptive feedback is given to students who fail to attend to mismatches between their self-assessments and their actual performance. Lastly, the Self-Assessment Tutor supports the entire problem-solving process, starting before students attempt to solve the target problem, and ending after students reflect on the solution.

Students begin the self-assessment process by predicting whether they could solve a given target problem without making errors (Question 1). Students reply by choosing either "yes" or "no, I need a hint", in which case a relevant hint is displayed. Both replies are legitimate, and no feedback is given on the students' initial self-assessment. Students are then asked to solve the target problem (Question 2). On this step, typical support is available (correctness feedback, error messages and on-demand hints). Question 3 asks students to recall their initial self-assessment and Question 4 asks students to reflect on whether they solved the target problem without making errors. Feedback on Questions 3 and 4 is given to ensure accurate recollection of students' initial self-assessment and actual ability. Question 5 is key in getting students to compare their initial self-assessment to their actual ability.

In response to the question "did you correctly evaluate your knowledge?", students can choose "yes", "no – I thought I knew it but was wrong", or "no – I knew more than I predicted". Feedback on this question was contingent on students' initial self-assessment and actual ability. For example, a student who estimated she could solve the target problem, yet failed to do so without errors, is expected to choose "no – I thought I knew it but was wrong". Lastly, students predict the need for help on new, similar, problems, by choosing either "yes, I will need the advice", or "no, I think I've got it" (Question 6). No feedback is given on this question.

The Self-Assessment Tutor is an example-tracing tutor and was built using the Cognitive Tutor Authoring Tools. In our study, the Self-Assessment Tutor was used in conjunction with the Geometry Cognitive Tutor. Each section of the Self-Assessment Tutor includes three to five problems, each of which targets a specific skill that is practiced in the subsequent section of the Geometry Cognitive Tutor. Students first evaluate their ability on the target set of problems in the Self-Assessment Tutor. Students then complete a sequence of problems that require the self-assessment skills, using the Geometry Cognitive Tutor.

The Self-Assessment Tutor was evaluated in a classroom study together with the Help Tutor. Participants were vocational tenth- and eleventh-grade high school students (n = 84) in five classrooms, taught by two teachers. All students were enrolled in the Cognitive Tutor Geometry class and thus were familiar with the Cognitive Tutor and its interface. Whole classes were assigned to conditions, balancing across conditions the number and level of students. Forty-six students in three classes were assigned to the self-assessment condition, while 38 students in the remaining two classes were assigned to the control condition.

Students in both conditions worked on two units from the Geometry Cognitive Tutor: Angles (Unit 1) and Quadrilaterals (Unit 2). Each of the units had a single warm-up problem, followed by three sections. Each section focused on a different set of skills within the general topic of the unit. Students in the control condition worked with the unmodified Geometry Cognitive Tutor, which did not include the Self-Assessment Tutor or the Help Tutor. Students in the self-assessment condition alternated between the Self-Assessment Tutor and the Geometry Cognitive Tutor augmented with the Help Tutor.

The study spanned three months. During Month 1 all students worked on Unit 1 in their respective conditions. During Month 2 the study was put on hold while students prepared for statewide exams using the unmodified Geometry Cognitive Tutor. During Month 3 students worked on Unit 2, again according to the conditions to which they had been assigned. Progress within each unit was at an individual pace.

On average, students worked with the Self-Assessment Tutor for 18 minutes. As it turned out, many students took longer than expected to complete sections 1.2 and 2.1 in the Geometry Cognitive Tutor and thus did not reach the more advanced sections. In Unit 1, all 46 students worked on Section 1.1, 37 students worked on Section 1.2 and only 14 students reached Section 1.3. In Unit 2, 44 students worked on Section 2.1 and only 12 and 2 students reached Sections 2.2 and 2.3 respectively.

Effect of Domain Knowledge. The Self-Assessment Tutor asks students to predict their ability to solve a target item (Question 1) and following their prediction to solve it (Question 2). Overall, students assessed their ability correctly on 77% of all problems. The accuracy of students' assessments depended on their knowledge level. There was a high significant correlation ($r = 0.52$) between having the relevant domain knowledge (as assessed by averaging performance on Question 2 on all items within each section) and making an accurate self-assessment on the self-assessment set of items. The relationship between having relevant domain-level knowledge and accuracy of self-assessment was most apparent when looking at the single item level. Students who had sufficient knowledge to solve the target item predicted their success (prior to attempting) on 84% of the items, while students who lacked sufficient knowledge to solve the target item predicted their failure (prior to attempting) on only 37% of the items. Thus, overestimation was much more common than underestimation.

Calibration of Self-Assessment. The Self-Assessment Tutor asks students to report their self-assessment twice for each skill: once before solving the target item (Question 1) and once after solving it (Question 6). Therefore, students could use their performance on the target item (Question 2) to calibrate their self-assessment. Students' updated self-assessment (Question 6) relied heavily on their initial self-assessment (Question 1), but was fine-tuned based on their actual performance (Question 2). The significant interaction shows that students who underestimated their ability updated their self-assessments more often than students who overestimated their ability. In fact, 77% of the students who thought they already knew how to solve the item did not update their self-assessments following their failure to solve the item. The high persistence of overestimation is especially noteworthy, given that a single failure is sufficient to suggest that the student does not possess sufficient knowledge.

Metacognitive Improvement. Due to the high attrition, and to avoid a selection bias, the improvement in students' self-assessment was evaluated only on sections in which attrition was low: Unit 1 Sections 1.1 and 1.2, and Unit 2 Section 2.1. Overall, students became more accurate in their initial self-assessments, as evaluated by comparing their self-assessments on Question 1 to their actual performance on Question 2. However, a likely explanation is that students' self-assessments improved because their domain knowledge increased. To control for the effect of domain learning, the accuracy of students' self-assessments was analyzed separately for items on which students had sufficient knowledge and items for which students lacked sufficient knowledge (as evaluated by performance on Question 2 in each problem). Students improved their self-assessment significantly from Section 1.1 (77%) to Section 1.2 (88%). There was also a positive trend from Section 1.1 to 2.1 (83%) on high-competence items. However, there was no improvement in the accuracy of students' self-assessments on items that they subsequently failed to solve correctly (Section 1.1: 37%; Section 1.2: 40%; Section 2.1: 39%). These results suggest that students got significantly better at identifying their strengths, but not their weaknesses.

Transfer of Self-Assessment Skills. To evaluate whether students transferred their improved ability to self-assess to an unsupported learning environment, students' self-assessments in the Self-Assessment Tutor were compared to their actual help-seeking behavior in the Geometry Cognitive Tutor. Specifically, the rate of asking for help in the Cognitive Tutor prior to attempting new problem-steps was examined. One would expect that students would seek more help in the Geometry Cognitive Tutor on skills for which they reported to have low self-assessment in the Self-Assessment Tutor. It was only natural that students would ask for more help on skills they did not know. However, as shown earlier, students were relatively poor at identifying their limitations.

The correlation between skills on which students sought more help in the Cognitive Tutor and skills on which students reported to have low initial self-assessment in the Self-Assessment Tutor was high and significant ($r = 0.75$). Other factors such as inherent difficulty or generic self-assessment skills may affect students' help-seeking behaviors within the Cognitive Tutor. These factors can be accounted for by partialing-out the corresponding help frequencies on the self-assessment skills of students in the control condition, who were susceptible to the self-assessment factors, yet did not work with the Self-Assessment Tutor. The partial correlation between help-requests in the Cognitive Tutor and reported need for help in the Self-Assessment Tutor, controlling for help-requests in the Cognitive Tutor by students in the control condition, remained high and significant: $r = 0.73$. This suggested that training with the Self-Assessment Tutor, rather than item difficulty or generic self-assessment skills, accounted for the high correlation between students' self-assessment and help-seeking behavior.

References

Brown, G. T. L., & Harris, L. R. (2013). Student self-assessment. In J. McMillan (Ed.), *The Sage Handbook of Research on Classroom Assessment* (pp. 367–393). Thousand Oaks, CA: Sage.

Dike, J. W., Mumuni, A. A. O., & Chinda, W. (2017). Metacognitive teaching strategies on secondary school students' academic performance. *International Journal of Computational Engineering Research (IJCER)*, *7*(1), 14–20.

Jacobson, N., & Viko, B. (2010). Effect of instruction in metacognitive self-assessment strategy on chemistry self-efficacy and achievement of senior secondary school students. *Academic Leadership: The Online Journal*, *8*(4), Article 19. https://scholars.fhsu.edu/alj/vol8/iss4/19

Kaderavek, J. N., Gillam, R. B., Ukrainetz, T. A., Justice, L. M., & Eisenberg, S. N. (2004). School-age children's self-assessment of oral narrative production. *Communication Disorders Quarterly*, *26*(1), 37–48. https://doi.org/10.1177/15257401040260010401

Kusuma, D., & Zaenuri, K. (2019). Creative thinking ability based on students' metacognition in creative problem-solving learning model with recitation and self-assessment in ethnomathematics. *Unnes Journal of Mathematics Education Research*, *8*(1), 25–34. https://journal.unnes.ac.id/sju/index.php/ujmer/article/view/2771

Panadero, E., & Romero, M. (2014). To rubric or not to rubric? The effects of self-assessment on self-regulation, performance and self-efficacy.

Assessment in Education: Principles, Policy & Practice, *21*(2), 133–148. doi: 10.1080/0969594X.2013.877872

Panadero, E., Jonsson, A., & Botella, J. (2017). Effects of self-assessment on self-regulated learning and self-efficacy: Four meta-analyses. *Educational Research Review*, *22*, 74–98. doi: https://doi.org/10.1016/j.edurev.2017.08.004

Roll, I., Aleven, V., McLaren, B. M., & Koedinger, K. R. (2011). Metacognitive practice makes perfect: Improving students' self-assessment skills with an intelligent tutoring system. In G. Biswas, S. Bull, J. Kay, & A. Mitrovic (Eds.), *Artificial Intelligence in Education. AIED 2011: Artificial Intelligence in Education: 15th International Conference*. Lecture Notes in Computer Science, vol. 6738. Berlin and Heidelberg: Springer. https://doi.org/10.1007/978-3-642-21869-9_38

Sitzmann, T., Ely, K., Brown, K. G., & Bauer, K. N. (2010). Self-assessment of knowledge: A cognitive learning or affective measure? *Academy of Management Learning & Education*, *9*(2), 169–191. https://doi.org/10.5465/amle.9.2.zqr169

14

Peer Assessment

Peer assessment involves students making judgments about the work of other students. Naturally, at first this seems strange, as students will be used to the teacher making such judgments. However, over time students become better at doing it. But as the view of just one student on your work may be unreliable (especially at first), teachers often have peer assessment groups of three or four students where everyone assesses everyone else's work, and then the peer assessments can be averaged. Additionally, peer assessments are not fixed and the person assessed decides what peer feedback to take on board and what to ignore. Peer assessments are often open to negotiation with the assessed and that metacognitive discourse heightens gains. Many researchers have found that being an assessor is actually more beneficial than being assessed. Of course, all of this takes time, so a teacher wanting to use peer assessment to save time might be disappointed. However, peer assessment can be just as reliable as teacher assessment.

Definition

Peer assessment is an arrangement for learners to consider and specify the level, value or quality of a product or performance of other equal-status learners. Other similar terms are used in the literature (e.g., peer grading/marking – giving a score to a peer product/performance; peer feedback – peers giving elaborated feedback; peer evaluation – more usually in workplaces regarding skill and knowledge; or peer review – more usually in academia regarding assessment of written papers). Several previous studies compared two or three types of peer assessment, but the variety in types goes far beyond that. O'Donnell and Topping (1998) described a typology of relevant variables, Gielen et al. (2011) offered a more developed inventory, and yet further developments came from Topping (2018), who outlined 43 variables.

Background

Zhan et al. (2023) conducted a meta-analysis of 56 papers on the effect of online peer assessment on higher-order thinking, but 56% of the papers were in higher education. The overall effect of online peer assessment on higher-order thinking was 0.76 (large). However, the effect size was larger for interventions in K-12 settings (ES = 0.98) than for those in higher education (ES = 0.65). It was found that the impact of online peer assessment on convergent thinking (ES = 0.97) was greater than the impact on divergent thinking (ES = 0.38). The effect size was considerably bigger when students both received and provided feedback (reciprocal peer assessment) (ES = 0.83) than when they only received it (ES = 0.11). With respect to anonymity, the overall effect size of anonymous online peer assessment (ES = 0.91) was higher than in studies not adopting it (ES = 0.59). When assessment criteria were given (perhaps in the form of a rubric), the effect size (ES = 0.78) was bigger than the effect size when students did not receive assessment criteria (ES = 0.44).

Turning to individual studies, teaching computer programming was challenging (Wang et al., 2017), but programming training could promote students' higher-order thinking performance. Several previous studies had attempted to develop user-friendly interfaces to ease students' cognitive loads. In this study, an online peer assessment-based system was developed, which students could use to provide comments to peers and review the feedback and scores from peers during the learning activity. A quasi-experiment was conducted with four classes (n = 166) of ninth graders in a junior high school. Two classes were assigned to the experimental group and two classes were the control group. The results showed that students in the experimental group had better programming knowledge and skills, as well as more positive learning attitudes and critical thinking awareness, than those in the control group.

Orluwene and Ekim (2020) investigated how self-regulated learning could be enhanced through the use of self- and peer-assessment techniques. The study used a sample of 145 third year secondary chemistry students from four schools. The four schools were assigned to three experimental groups (self-assessment, peer assessment and a combination of self- and peer assessment) and one control group (teacher assessment). Pre-test and post-test data were collected using a 22-item Self-Regulated Learning Scale with responses on a four-point Likert scale. This instrument had validity of 0.79 and internal consistency of 0.86. Results showed that self-assessment, peer assessment and a combination of self- and peer assessment were all effective in promoting self-regulated learning. However, the combination of self- and peer-assessment techniques was the most effective, followed by self-assessment only, then peer assessment only and lastly teacher assessment.

The influence of self-assessment and peer assessment in fostering students' engagement and improving metacognitive skills was investigated by Ybyrayeva and Koshkarova (2023). A mixed-methods approach, incorporating both quantitative surveys and qualitative interviews, was used. A diverse student sample (n = 500) from four high schools was surveyed using adapted versions of the Motivated Strategies for Learning Questionnaire and the Metacognitive Awareness Inventory before and after the implementation of a structured program incorporating self-assessment and peer-assessment strategies. Additionally, 40 students were selected for semi-structured interviews to gain deeper insights into their experiences. Quantitative findings showed a significant increase in students' scores on both questionnaires following the implementation of self-assessment and peer-assessment strategies, indicating improved engagement and metacognitive skills. Qualitative data corroborated these findings, with students expressing increased awareness of their learning processes and a deeper engagement with the material. The results showed a significant positive correlation between the implementation of self-assessment and peer-assessment strategies and enhanced student engagement, as well as improved metacognitive skills.

Specimen Program

Chang et al. (2021) note that STEM (science, technology, engineering and mathematics) refers to a cross-disciplinary learning design for engaging students in applying integrated knowledge to complete a project or solve a complex problem. However, STEM tasks are complex and challenging to students. To help students understand teachers' rating standards, increase the opportunity to observe and receive feedback on peers' work, and improve their cognitive level and higher-order thinking such as critical thinking, this study used a peer-assessment approach.

A quasi-experiment was conducted in a junior high school in Taiwan with four classes of 112 students with average age 12. The experimental group (two classes with 53 students) learned with the peer-assessment (PA) approach, while the control group (two classes with 59 students) used the conventional STEM approach. Results showed that the experimental group students had significantly higher learning achievement, collaboration tendency, critical thinking awareness, problem solving and metacognition than controls. Peer-assessment scores were highly correlated with teacher-assessment scores, indicating that students were able to provide accurate ratings of their peers' STEM work.

In each class, the participants were divided into small teams of four or five to collaboratively complete the project. Both groups of students were taught by the same teacher. Instruments included a pre- and post-test of learning achievement, rubrics for assessing the project work, and collaboration tendency, critical thinking awareness, problem-solving tendency and metacognition tendency questionnaires. The peer-assessment rubrics consisted of four dimensions: construction, accuracy, cognition and innovation. Each questionnaire used a five-point Likert-type rating scheme (1 = strongly disagree; 5 = strongly agree). The items of the scales are listed in the Implementation section below. The collaboration tendency questionnaire had a reliability of 0.89. The critical thinking awareness questionnaire had six questions with a reliability of 0.71. The problem-solving tendency measure had six questions and a reliability of 0.78. The metacognition tendency questionnaire had five questions and a reliability of 0.83.

Results revealed a significant difference in the post-test achievement scores of the two groups ($p<0.001$), with the post-test score of the experimental group being significantly higher than that of the control group. The collaboration tendency, critical thinking awareness, problem-solving tendency and metacognition tendency of the experimental group were significantly higher than those of the control group. The correlation between students' learning achievement and metacognition tendency ($r = 0.20$) was also statistically significant.

Implementation

It is generally challenging for teachers to design learning tasks that take multiple disciplines into account and to examine students' learning achievements in interdisciplinary tasks, although interdisciplinarity is an important approach to linking core cognitive skills to enhance students' higher-order thinking. In interdisciplinary STEM activities, the teacher is not a distributor of knowledge but rather a supervisor and regulator of learning activities to develop students' ability to integrate knowledge and form solutions.

Extensive research has shown that interdisciplinary STEM courses produce better student learning achievement than traditional single course instruction. A well-designed STEM curriculum not only allows students to develop practical skills, but also encourages them to be more active in interactive behaviors such as investigation, communication and collaboration.

STEM can induce students to think through questions or situations and enhances students' affective outcomes, such as learning interest and learning motivation.

Also, by comparing peers' work and giving feedback, students' higher-order thinking such as critical thinking awareness and metacognition tendency can be enhanced. Mathematics is considered the foundation of all other sciences, but students are commonly taught to solve mathematics problems (such as equations, geometry and graphs) in a form not linked to practical application contexts.

The process of comparing other people's work from different points of view can be called reflective knowledge construction. Peer assessment might help students perceive what they have learned, as well as supporting them in making their own reflections on and improvements in their learning tasks. However, especially for inexperienced learners, using peer assessment in complex learning activities could impose a high cognitive load. Assessment rubrics that clearly state the specified dimensions and rating criteria are likely to be helpful. Higher-order thinking is important in peer assessment. Collaboration means the ability to interact with others via sharing ideas, to make reflections, resolve conflicts and reconstruct knowledge to complete learning tasks.

The STEM activities in this study were based on the Pythagorean Theorem unit in a middle school mathematics course. The purpose of this activity was to teach students the relationship between the lengths of the three sides of a triangle. The basic concepts of rotation, angle and symmetry were also taught. The process of graphical drawing was conducted using the GeoGebra online platform. GeoGebra is a free mathematical tool that can be used to design, draw, display, and submit 3D graphics. The interface of the software allows students to enter and set the type of shape anywhere in the coordinate system or to insert a local image for creation. Students can set up different stages of shape changes, including panning, rotation, symmetry and so on.

A simple shape could be transformed into a complex shape by cutting and rotating. For example, two small squares are transformed by splitting them just enough to fill a large square. The edge length of these three squares can form the three sides of a right triangle, which explains the Pythagorean Theorem. Also, the triangle can be transformed into a bird pattern by using curves and rotation. The students' task was to convert simple shapes into complex collage patterns.

In terms of science literacy, these activities incorporated computational thinking, where students were taught to describe and create through observation and recording. In terms of technology literacy, students were asked to use painting software to create a collage on the computer and to use the principle of slider animation to demonstrate their creativity. In terms of engineering literacy, students had the opportunity to use the painting software and to operate the laser cutter to cut materials. In terms of mathematics literacy, the goal of this course was to provide students with a basic understanding of the Pythagorean Theorem and the principles of angle measurement, rotation, and symmetry in the design and creation of geometric figures.

The peer feedback system was implemented on the Zuvio platform, an online environment that allows teachers to collect students' ratings and comments (e.g., on peers' projects or reports), as well as collecting students' answers to a set of questions related to an issue. The system enabled students to score peers' projects using smartphones based on the rubrics provided by the teacher after watching peers' projects displayed on a desktop computer. After students logged into the platform, a group list was provided so that they could select the evaluation target in the display sequence. The students then needed to enter the corresponding interface to give scores or comments.

In the rating stage, students were engaged in comparing the four dimensions of each project and then rating them based on their strengths and weaknesses. Finally, students needed to provide comments for peers to revise their works. After each stage of peer review, a group of students could read peers' feedback using a smartphone and revise their work on a computer. Teacher assessment was conducted on the same platform and based on the same procedure as the peer assessment.

The project lasted for three weeks, with two 50-minute sessions per week. In the first week, the teacher led the students to complete the pre-test questionnaire and learning achievement test. The questionnaire items are listed below:

Collaboration tendency

1. In a team activity, I believe that all of the team members will try their best to complete the task.
2. In a team activity, I believe our team will successfully collaborate to complete the task.
3. When my peers propose some ideas, I will not question their motives.
4. When collaborating with peers, I generally communicate with them well.
5. When collaborating with peers, we generally have the tasks properly assigned to each of the team members.

Critical thinking awareness

1. In this class, I think about whether what I've learned is correct.
2. In this class, I will judge the value of new information or evidence presented to me.
3. In this class, I think about other possible ways of understanding what I am learning.
4. In this class, I consider different opinions to see which one makes more sense.
5. In this class, I can tell what information can be trusted.
6. In this class, I provide reasons and evidence for my opinions.

Problem-solving tendency

1. I believe that I have the ability to solve the problems I encounter.
2. I believe that I can solve problems on my own.
3. I have experiences of solving the problems I encounter.
4. When encountering problems, I am willing to face and deal with them.

5. I will not escape from the problems I encounter.
6. I always try my best to solve the problems I encounter.

Metacognition tendency
1. I ask myself periodically if I am meeting my goal.
2. I periodically review to help me understand important relationships.
3. I find myself pausing regularly to check my comprehension.
4. I ask myself how well I accomplished my goals once I'm finished.
5. I ask myself if I learned as much as I could have, once I finish a task.

Before the activity began, the prerequisite knowledge of the Pythagorean Theorem was reviewed to ensure that both groups could successfully complete the collage. Subsequently, the teacher used GeoGebra to demonstrate completion of a collage to familiarize students with the use of the platform. Students were then free to use their imagination to create works with diverse ideas.

In the second week, the groups of students discussed questions and then worked on their STEM project. Students in the experimental group were graded by peer assessment. Each student was asked to evaluate the projects developed by other teams in the same class, i.e., six or seven projects. Students then made modifications and adjustments based on the feedback and suggestions. Students in the control group were evaluated by the teacher and made modifications and adjustments based on the teacher's comments.

The revised projects were presented in the last week. At this point, the experimental group students conducted peer assessment again, while the control group students were evaluated by the teacher. The teacher then introduced how to use the laser cutter and selected outstanding works from each team. The students were guided to use the laser cutter to complete their artifacts.

Finally, the students were asked to complete a post-test questionnaire and a learning achievement post-test.

References

Chang, D., Hwang, G. J., Chang, S. C., & Wang, S. Y. (2021). Promoting students' cross-disciplinary performance and higher order thinking: A peer assessment-facilitated STEM approach in a mathematics course. *Education Technology Research and Development*, 69, 3281–3306. https://doi.org/10.1007/s11423-021-10062-z

Gielen, S., Dochy, F., & Onghena, P. (2011). An inventory of peer assessment diversity. *Assessment and Evaluation in Higher Education*, 36(2), 137–155. https://doi.org/10.1080/02602930903221444

O'Donnell, A., & Topping, K. J. (1998). Peers assessing peers: Possibilities and problems. In K. Topping & S. Ehly (Eds.), *Peer-Assisted Learning*. Mahwah, NJ: Lawrence Erlbaum.

Orluwene, G. W., & Ekim, R. D. E. (2020). Promoting self-regulated learning through self- and peer-assessments techniques among secondary school students. *International Journal of Arts and Commerce*, 9(4), 1–16.

Topping, K. J. (2018). *Using Peer Assessment to Inspire Reflection and Learning*. Student Assessment for Educators Series (Ed. J. H. MacMillan). New York and London: Routledge. www.routledge.com/9780815367659 (also published in translation in Chinese by Zhejiang University Press).

Wang, X. M., Hwang, G. J., Liang, Z. Y., & Wang, H. Y. (2017). Enhancing students' computer programming performances, critical thinking awareness and attitudes towards programming: An online peer-assessment attempt. *Educational Technology & Society*, 20(4), 58–68. https://www.jstor.org/stable/10.2307/26229205

Ybyrayeva, K., & Koshkarova, U. (2023). The role of self-assessment and peer assessment in promoting students' engagement and meta cognitive skills. *Scientific Collection "InterConf"*, 157, 106–108. Proceedings of the 2nd International Scientific and Practical

Conference "Science: Development and Factors in Its Influence" (June 6–8, 2023). Amsterdam, Netherlands. https://archive.interconf.center/index.php/conference-proceeding/article/view/3763

Zhan, Y., Yan, Z., Wan, Z. H., Wang, X., Zeng, Y., Yang, M., & Yang, L. (2023). Effects of online peer assessment on higher-order thinking: A meta-analysis. *British Journal of Educational Technology*, *54*, 817–835. doi: 10.1111/bjet.13310

Section C

Programs Focusing Especially on Self-Regulated Learning

15
Metacognition and Decision Making

From a metacognitive point of view, as we proceed from metacognitive knowledge to metacognitive skills and begin to develop self-regulation, the extent to which we can deploy all these to help make better decisions becomes important. Decisions can have a profound influence on one's pathway in life, although of course there are very small decisions and very large ones.

Definition

Decision making is the cognitive process leading to the selection of a belief or a course of action among several possible alternative options. It could be either rational or irrational, the result of extensive reflection or very little. Nearly every decision we make will affect ourselves and other people in one way or another. It's important to be aware of the influence our decisions will have, and understand what the human cost will be. The decisions we make demonstrate our values.

Factors and personal characteristics that have an impact on decision making include: programmed versus non-programmed decisions, information inputs, prejudice, cognitive constraints, attitudes about risk and uncertainty, personal habits, and social and cultural influences. Indecision can sometimes become decision by default – if you decide not to decide, you effectively decide to give up your power of choice.

The DECIDE model is the acronym of six particular activities needed in the decision-making process: (1) D = define the problem, (2) E = establish the criteria, (3) C = consider all the alternatives, (4) I = identify the best alternative, (5) D = develop and implement a plan of action, and (6) E = evaluate and monitor the effects of the action. This is of course a mnemonic (see Chapter 12).

Background

Zhou et al. (2022) offered a meta-analysis of metacognition and academic procrastination. Insofar as procrastination reflects an inability to make a decision (even to start), this seems relevant here. Procrastination can be regarded as a failure of self-regulation. Almost all people suffer from a degree of procrastination in their everyday lives, but academic procrastination is a tendency to put off starting, continuing with or finishing academic tasks, which might be reading, writing, discussing, presenting or so forth. It refers to a tendency to delay an intended course of study-related action despite the negative consequences of such a delay, whether that tendency is implicit or explicit.

Metacognition plays an essential role in explaining and predicting procrastination and might reduce procrastination. Extensive research has been conducted investigating what factors are likely to result in procrastination, including personality, boredom, coping strategy, achievement goals, perceived parenting style and so forth. Engagement in worry and rumination drains mental resources, reducing the ability to perform. Male students tend to procrastinate more.

"Active procrastination" denotes a conscious delay whereby an individual intentionally postpones his/her action and subsequently benefits from it, reflecting an individual's preference for time pressure, intentional decision to procrastinate, capacity to meet deadlines and ability to achieve satisfactory outcomes.

"Passive procrastination" by contrast implies a subconscious delay where decisions are avoided rather than deferred.

Zhou et al.'s study reviewed past empirical findings on the relationship between metacognition and procrastination. Fifty-nine relevant articles involving a total of 23,627 participants were synthesized. Results showed significant small effect sizes of metacognition for passive procrastination (0.28), but not for active procrastination (0.03). Further, different dimensions of metacognition showed different relational patterns with procrastination. In particular, metacognitive belief and metacognitive regulation were significantly associated with passive procrastination; however, metacognition (regardless of type) was not significantly associated with active procrastination. After controlling for grade level, individualism and gender, no significant moderation effects were found for either active or passive procrastination.

Turning to individual studies, Eggert et al. (2013) examined the effects of cooperative training strategies to enhance students' socio-scientific decision making and metacognitive skills in science. Socio-scientific decision making referred to both describing socio-scientific issues and developing and evaluating solutions to socio-scientific issues. Two cooperative training strategies were investigated, which differed with respect to embedded metacognitive instructions. Participants were 360 senior high school students who studied either in a cooperative learning setting, a cooperative learning setting with embedded metacognitive questions, or a nontreatment control group. Results indicated that students in the two training conditions outperformed students in the control group on both processes of socio-scientific decision making. However, students in the cooperative learning plus metacognitive questions condition did not outperform students in the cooperative learning condition. With respect to students' learning outcomes on self-regulation, all conditions improved over time, but students in the cooperative learning plus metacognition condition scored highest at post-test.

Keshavarzi et al. (2017) investigated the effect of metacognitive awareness on decision-making styles and emotion regulation in female high school students. Two classes were randomly assigned to experimental (n = 19) and control (n = 19) groups. A metacognitive awareness intervention program was carried out over eight sessions (once a week for 90 minutes) for the experimental group, but the control group did not receive any intervention. The Decision Styles Questionnaire and the Regulation of Emotion Questionnaire were administered. Compared with the control group, results showed a significant decrease in scores on the avoidant, anxious, intuitive and spontaneous dimensions for the experimental group, as well as a significant increase in the score on decision-making styles. Moreover, the scores on the dysfunction dimension of emotion regulation decreased significantly in the experimental group, while the scores on the function dimension increased significantly.

A study was conducted to determine third and fourth grade primary school students' metacognitive awareness and perception of their decision-making skill, and the relationship between them (Akaydıni et al., 2020). The random sample of 143 students was of third and fourth grade primary school students attending state schools. As data collection tools, the Teacher Form to Determine Primary School Students' Metacognitive Awareness and the Scale of Third and Fourth Grade Primary School Students' Perception of Decision-Making Skill were used. The findings showed that primary school students' metacognitive awareness and perception of their decision-making skill were high. Neither showed gender or grade level differences. A positive correlation between the students' metacognitive awareness and their perception of decision-making skill was found. Their metacognitive awareness was found to predict their perception of decision-making skill. Thus, when teachers engage students in metacognitive activities, their decision-making skill can also be developed.

From a different perspective, von Gillern and Stufft (2023) examined how 31 middle school children conducted multimodal analyses of video games. Over four consecutive days, students played video games for 30 minutes and then wrote written reflections about the multimodal symbols within the game – and how these symbols influenced their interpretation and decision-making processes during gameplay. The students produced 124 reflections in total, which were analyzed to determine how children metacognitively reflected on different types of multimodal symbols and used those symbols to comprehend the games and make decisions. Results illustrated how students engaged in metacognitive semantic and syntactic processes with a variety of multimodal symbols during gameplay, such as written language, dynamic visuals and abstract symbols, that aided their understanding of the games and influenced their decisions. This study illustrated children's meaning-making processes while engaged with video games as multimodal interactive texts.

Specimen Program

Moses-Payne et al. (2021) noted that adolescents aspire for independence. Adolescence is a time when becoming independent from one's parents is particularly pertinent, as adolescents feel a need for increasing control over their own decisions. Becoming an independent decision maker is an important step towards full adult autonomy. However, resistance to authority and increased risk-taking behaviors during this period have sometimes suggested that adolescents still lack the necessary abilities for making good independent decisions.

Inter alia, successful independence means knowing when to rely on one's own knowledge and when to listen to others. A critical prerequisite is well-developed metacognitive ability to accurately assess the quality of one's own knowledge. This metacognitive ability – the ability to accurately introspect on one's own decisions – is critical when deciding how much to rely on one's own decisions or on the advice of others. The study distinguished between participants' overall confidence (metacognitive bias) and ability to track performance (metacognitive sensitivity). By combining metacognition and advice taking in one task, it was possible to investigate how young people could utilize their emerging metacognitive abilities to arbitrate between helpful and misleading advice.

The interaction between confidence and advice taking was assessed in children (8–9 years), early adolescents (12–13 years) and late adolescents (16–17 years). Participants from multiple schools (n = 107) were recruited, 45 male and 62 female, in three age groups: age 8–9 (n = 30), age 12–13 (n = 41) and age 16–17 (n = 36). Schools were selected from socially diverse and disadvantaged areas.

Participants were introduced to the Space Explorer task and given both verbal and written instructions. Participants also completed three other tasks, some questionnaires and the Wechsler Abbreviated Scale of Intelligence (WASI-II) verbal and abstract reasoning tests. They were tested in groups of three to four. The order in which participants completed the tasks, questionnaires and WASI-II was randomized between participants. In total, the adolescent participants (12–13 years, 16–17 years) spent about 1.5 hours completing the experiment. The youngest participants (8–9 years) completed the experiment over two sessions to reduce fatigue (however, the Space Explorer task was always completed within a single session), and spent about two hours completing the experiment.

This study showed that metacognition matures from childhood to adolescence and coincides with greater independent decision making. Adolescents, in contrast to children, take on others' advice less often, but this only when the advice is misleading. It was also shown that adolescents' reduced reliance on others' advice is explained by their increased metacognitive skills, suggesting that a developing ability to introspect may support independent decision making in adolescence.

Implementation

In the Space Explorer task, participants viewed a spaceship cockpit, within which were two display screens (one central for displaying choice, one to the side for displaying advice) and a confidence slider (displayed only during confidence reports). Stimuli for the perceptual decision consisted of a planet, presented briefly in the center of the screen, with 68 aliens displayed in circle formation over the top of the planet. There were eight possible alien colors (selected to be easily discriminated between, even by participants with color blindness), but on each trial two different color aliens were randomly selected. Aliens were identical apart from differences in color. There was always more of one color alien than the other, and the exact difference in number was calibrated to individual participants to ensure equal performance. After stimulus presentation, an example of the two aliens was displayed on the left and right of the central display screen for participants to make their choice.

Participants were first asked to make a perceptual decision based on an array of two different color aliens presented for 750 milliseconds. Participants were instructed to decide as quickly as possible ("as quickly as you can") which of the two aliens there was more of and log their response by key press. This was followed by a confidence rating. Participants rated their confidence on a sliding scale from "total guess" to "totally certain", chosen after piloting to ensure the youngest participants would comprehend the scale. In half of the trials, this was then followed by advice from a "space advisor". The advised answer (an image of one alien) was displayed to participants for 1500 milliseconds in a small "messenger screen". Participants were then given the option to revise their initial choice and re-rated their confidence.

The advice was correct on 70% of trials. This level of accuracy of advice was chosen in order to avoid stereotyped responses from the participants (advice that is totally accurate may lead participants to always follow advice and ignore their own choices, whereas advice that is random may lead to participants completely ignoring it). The trials on which advice was given and on which the advice was correct or incorrect (70% correct trials) were randomly determined. Participants were verbally instructed that "the advisor should be correct most of the time but can also make mistakes" (and this was reiterated in the written instructions, given by a masked astronaut: "the advisor should be correct most of the time, but they're only human, so can make mistakes just like you and I!").

For the practice trials (first 30 trials), participants simply made the perceptual decision and were given feedback ("correct" vs. "incorrect"). There was no evidence that the amount of positive versus negative feedback in the practice trials had an influence on confidence-related measures in the main task. Feedback was given on practice trials to allow faster convergence and so that the researchers could monitor performance to ensure participants understood the task. In the remaining 80 trials, participants were no longer given feedback but instead rated their confidence in their response. For half of these trials, participants received advice, revised their initial choice and re-rated their confidence. All pre- and post-advice decisions and confidence ratings were self-paced. In total, the Space Explorer task took 10–20 minutes to complete.

A staircase procedure was used throughout the task. A 2-down-1-up staircase procedure that converged at 70% accuracy was used to identify the difference in aliens needed to elicit near-threshold performance (i.e., between chance and ceiling performance) for individual participants, so as to elicit the most variation in confidence ratings. The staircase would also account for any differences in speed-accuracy trade-offs between groups by adjusting evidence strength accordingly. Metacognitive bias was calculated by taking the mean confidence rating across all trials in which confidence ratings were given. Given that basic task performance was equated between subjects, mean confidence ratings revealed between-subject "bias" in subjective confidence (rating generally high or low confidence).

Overall propensity to follow advice was calculated by taking the proportion of trials where participants switched their choice when the advisor disagreed with them (over total number of trials where the advisor disagreed) minus the proportion of trials where participants switched their choice when the advisor agreed with them (over total number of trials where the advisor agreed). This was done to account for changes of mind that were not advice-related.

Resistance to false advice was calculated by taking the proportion of trials in which participants followed helpful advice and switched to the advised correct choice (over the total number of trials where participants were incorrect and received conflicting advice), minus the proportion of trials in which participants followed misleading advice and switched to the advised incorrect choice (over the total number of trials where participants were correct and received conflicting advice).

Participants did not differ in their overall task performance, nor at any point during the task. Age groups did not differ in IQ and IQ did not relate to any task-based measures. Confidence ratings were well distributed and were similarly variable across age groups. Metacognitive bias peaked significantly in the 12–13 years group, showing that this age group was more confident than the other groups. Males were also significantly more confident than females. Whilst metacognitive bias provides information about overall confidence, it does not provide any information about how well confidence ratings were calibrated to participants' actual performance. Metacognitive efficiency, on the other hand, measures how well participants' confidence ratings aligned with their performance.

There was an improvement in metacognitive efficiency in an adolescent-emergent pattern across age groups. Both adolescent groups (12–13-year-olds and 16–17-year-olds) had significantly better metacognitive efficiency than the pre-adolescent group (8–9-year-olds).

This means the confidence reports given by the adolescent groups were better calibrated to their actual performance than the confidence reports given by the pre-adolescent group.

The difference between the proportion of trials where participants changed their minds when the advisor disagreed versus when the advisor agreed with them was calculated. An (inverse) adolescent-emergent pattern was found, showing that the adolescent participants generally followed advice less than the youngest participants. The adolescent groups, compared with the youngest group, were more resistant to false advice and more willing to follow helpful advice. So far, two parallel age-related effects were observed. Adolescents had better metacognition (i.e., were better able to take account of their own performance) when deciding whether to follow advice. In addition, adolescents were better at arbitrating between their own decision and others' advice. As to whether emerging metacognition was the driving factor behind improved advice taking, the mediation analysis confirmed significant associations between adolescent-emergent age and metacognitive efficiency and between adolescent-emergent age and resistance to false advice. Moreover, there was a significant association between metacognitive efficiency and resistance to false advice. The association between adolescent-emergent age and resistance to false advice was fully mediated by metacognitive efficiency. The association between adolescent-emergent age and resistance to false advice was no longer significant when accounting for metacognitive efficiency.

This pattern of results showed that adolescents' ability to more accurately identify when they were correct and when they were incorrect allowed them to ignore advice more often when it was misleading but incorporate advice when it was helpful. In contrast, children were less able to identify when they were correct or incorrect and so tended to follow conflicting advice independent of their own performance and whether the advice was helpful or misleading. This suggests that adolescents do not simply ignore advice from others but use their confidence signals to guide their advice-taking behavior.

References

Akaydını, B. B., Yorulmaz, A., & Çokçalışkan, H. (2020). Investigation of primary school students' metacognitive awareness and decision-making skill. *International Journal of Progressive Education*, *16*(4), 158–171. doi: 10.29329/ijpe.2020.268.10

Eggert, S., Ostermeyer, F., Hasselhorn, M., & Bögeholz, S. (2013). Socio-scientific decision making in the science classroom: The effect of embedded metacognitive instructions on students' learning outcomes. *Education Research International*, vol. 2013, 309894. http://dx.doi.org/10.1155/2013/309894

Keshavarzi, S., MirNasab, M., Fathi Azar, E., & Badri Gargari, R. A. (2017). Effects of a metacognitive awareness program on high school students' decision-making styles and emotion regulation. *Journal of Cognitive Psychology*, *5*(1), 55–65.

Moses-Payne, M. E., Habicht, J., Bowler, A., Steinbeis, N., & Hauser, T. U. (2021). I know better! Emerging metacognition allows adolescents to ignore false advice. *Developmental Science*, *24*, e13101. doi: 10.1111/desc.13101

von Gillern, S., & Stufft, C. (2023). Multimodality, learning and decision-making: Children's metacognitive reflections on their engagement with video games as interactive texts. *Literacy*, *57*(1), 3–16. https://doi.org/10.1111/lit.12304

Zhou, M. M., Lam, K. K. L., & Zhang, Y. J. (2022). Metacognition and academic procrastination: A meta-analytical examination. *Journal of Rational-Emotive & Cognitive-Behavior Therapy*, *40*, 334–368. https://doi.org/10.1007/s10942-021-00415-1

16

Self-Regulation and Metacognitive Skills

Self-regulation of learning develops from the application of metacognitive skills, but has grown to be a field of study in its own right. Indeed, the *Handbook of Self-Regulation* was published as long ago as the year 2000 (with another by Zimmerman and Schunk in 2011 and a second edition by Schunk and Greene in 2018). This is why this chapter is rather large.

Definition

Self-regulated learning (SRL) refers to one's ability to understand and control one's learning environment. Self-regulation abilities include goal-setting, self-monitoring, self-instruction, and self-reinforcement. A self-regulated learner monitors, directs and regulates actions toward goals of information acquisition, expanding expertise and self-improvement.

Pintrich (2000) believed SRL had four phases: (1) forethought, planning and activation; (2) monitoring; (3) control; and (4) reaction and reflection. He described self-regulated learning as "an active, constructive process whereby learners set goals for their learning and then attempt to monitor, regulate, and control their cognition, motivation and behavior, guided and constrained by their goals and the contextual features in the environment" (p. 453).

Different elements stand out in this definition. First, there is an active part: students are actively involved and have clear intentions to be engaged in learning. This links directly to the second element: goal-orientation, i.e., the purposeful focus of learning on the achievement of a goal. The third aspect, the regulation and control of cognition, refers to the use of learning strategies to enhance one's learning. The fourth element relates to the context. A learning environment can stimulate or hinder learning (e.g., working in a quiet, orderly space instead of a chaotic and noisy room). The final element is student motivation: students have to be motivated to adopt this intense form of learning, in which motivational and cognitive aspects are intertwined. In short, self-regulated learning is a complex process, containing cognitive, motivational and contextual elements.

In fact, there are several models of SRL, but most of them include a preparatory phase, a performance phase and an appraisal phase, each consisting of different sub-processes. Panadero (2017) analyzed and compared six models of SRL – Zimmerman; Boekaerts; Winne and Hadwin; Pintrich; Efklides; and Hadwin, Järvelä and Miller – finding that different definitions reflected development in different ages and stages.

SRL is important in relation to transfer of learning or generalization (Perkins & Salomon, 1992). Transfer of learning occurs when learning in one context enhances (positive transfer) or undermines (negative transfer) a related performance in another context. Transfer includes near transfer (to closely related contexts and performances) and far transfer (to rather different contexts and performances). Research on transfer finds that very often transfer does not occur, especially "far" transfer. Findings suggest that transfer happens by way of two rather different mechanisms. Reflexive or low road transfer involves the triggering of well-practiced routines by stimulus conditions similar to those in the learning context. Mindful or high road transfer involves deliberate effortful abstraction and a search for connections. Conventional educational practices often fail to establish the conditions either for reflexive or mindful transfer.

Background

Reviews and Meta-Analyses

A number of previous meta-analyses have investigated the influence of SRL on student learning and performance. Dignath et al. (2008) offered a meta-analysis of primary/elementary self-regulation training programs in elementary schools, considering academic achievement, cognitive and metacognitive strategy application, and motivation. Results from 48 comparisons from 30 articles yielding 2631 effect sizes showed that SRL interventions were effective at the primary school level (effect size for academic performance = 0.62). Effect sizes for mathematics were higher for reading. The use of cognitive and metacognitive strategies yielded a mean effect size of 0.73. For motivational aspects (including self-efficacy) the mean effect size was even higher (0.76). Group work also had a high effect size.

In a later study, Dignath and Büttner (2008) encompassed both primary (49 studies) and secondary (35 studies) school (357 effect sizes in total). The mean effect size for academic performance was 0.61 for primary school and 0.54 for secondary school. However, the effect size for motivational aspects was considerably lower for secondary students. For both school levels, effect sizes were higher when the training was conducted by researchers instead of regular teachers. Interventions in mathematics had higher effect sizes than those in reading/writing or other subjects.

Sitzmann and Ehly (2011) investigated 16 different SRL components. Meta-analytic findings supported theoretical propositions that self-regulation constructs were interrelated – 30% of the correlations among constructs were .50 or greater. Goal level, persistence, effort and self-efficacy were the self-regulation constructs with the strongest effects on learning, accounting for 17% of the variance in learning. However, other self-regulatory processes did not exhibit significant relationships with learning.

A systematic analysis by de Boer et al. (2012) had 55 studies selected, involving 95 interventions, of which 23 focused on reading comprehension, 16 on writing, 44 on mathematics, nine on science and three on other subjects. Interventions were implemented in grades 2 to 11. Most interventions were implemented by the teacher, but in 15 cases by computer. On average, interventions took 13 weeks, with 2.3 sessions a week. There was an average effect size of 0.66 (reading comprehension 0.36, writing 1.25, mathematics and science 0.66 and 0.73 respectively). Longer interventions had slightly smaller effects on student performance than shorter interventions. Strategy instruction in general metacognitive knowledge, planning and prediction, rehearsal or task value produced significantly higher effects than strategy instruction that did not include these strategies. For 18 interventions, maintenance effects were measured, on average after 12.5 weeks. Follow-up effects were slightly higher than post-test effects.

As noted above, Panadero (2017) analyzed and compared six models of SRL. There were differential effects of SRL models in light of differences in students' developmental stages or educational levels. Panadero helpfully gives measurement instruments for each model discussed.

Efklides and Metallidou (2020) found interactions between metacognition and affect, so that metacognitive control decisions were based not only on the task demands of cognitive processing, but also on students' affective experiences and motivation. Meta-analytic evidence suggested that SRL could be cultivated in educational contexts in preschool and primary education. Most of the interventions resulted in significant overall effects on academic performance. The magnitude of these effect sizes was moderated by various student, training and context-related factors.

Self-regulation interventions were typically comprised of cognitive learning strategies, mnemonic strategies and/or behavioral management strategies (Elhusseini et al., 2022). A meta-analysis focused on interventions in primary and secondary students' mathematics, reading and writing outcomes. A total of 46 studies were included. There was an overall positive effect of self-regulation interventions on academic outcomes, suggesting that self-regulation interventions can lead to improved reading, writing and mathematics scores for children and adolescents.

Turning now to reviews which focused on narrower areas of education, Muir et al. (2023) investigated interventions in preschool settings, identifying 85 studies in a systematic analysis. Some intervention approaches had more consistent and robust evidence of efficacy (e.g., mindfulness, mediated play, physical activity). Across intervention approaches, some characteristics had greater presence amongst the higher-efficacy interventions (e.g., cognitive challenge and movement, as well as interventionist, fidelity and dose considerations).

There are two reviews of SRL in learning computer programming. Prather et al. (2020) conducted a systematic review discussing eight common theories of SRL. They also highlighted 11 theories on related constructs (e.g., self-efficacy) used to understand programming education. Seven instruments and protocols measuring metacognition and self-regulation had been used (the Motivated Strategies for Learning Questionnaire, Classroom Assessment Techniques, Self-Efficacy Scales, Self-Regulation Questionnaires, Student Perceptions of Classroom Knowledge Building, Epistemological Beliefs Questionnaire and Achievement Goal Framework Questionnaire). No effect sizes were calculated.

Loksa et al. (2022) also offered a systematic review of metacognition and self-regulation in computer programming, making new observations about the way theories are used by the computing education community. In particular, exemplars of studies that had used existing theories to support their design and discussion of results are discussed, as well as studies that had proposed their own metacognitive theories in the context of programming education.

There are also two studies on SRL in an online environment. A meta-analysis was conducted by Xu et al. (2022) of 50 papers on metacognition in an online and/or blended environment in elementary, secondary and higher education settings. Consistent with previously published meta-analyses of offline metacognition, a positive and moderate effect of SRL intervention (ES = 0.69) on learners' academic achievement in online and blended environments was confirmed. Studies from STEM (n = 51) had a larger effect size (.88; non-STEM n = 40, ES = 0.40). The online course/online learning system (n = 55) produced the largest effect size (.72), the blended learning context (n = 9) came next (.55), the web-based learning context next (n = 23, ES = 0.52), and the smallest effect size was for the mobile learning context (n = 5, ES = 0.41). Elementary education (n = 7) produced the largest effect size (2.21), higher education (n = 60) ES = 0.58, and secondary education (n = 23) ES = 0.43. Neither the intervention's duration nor intensity yielded significant differences in effect size.

A meta-analysis of research was conducted on the relationship between learning analytics (LA) and online self-regulated learning (OSRL) (Yu & Zhang, 2023). Twenty-two studies were included. Results indicated that (1) learning analytics had a positive effect (ES =0.97) on online self-regulated learning, (2) relationship mining had a larger effect on online self-regulated learning compared with clustering and distillation of data for human judgment, (3) log data was a critical method of collecting information in that it had a larger effect on OSRL compared with questionnaires, and (4) the effect size for undergraduate students was larger than that for K-12 and graduate.

Individual Studies
Turning to individual studies, Stoeger et al. (2014) examined the impact of a teacher-led intervention, implemented during regular classroom instruction and homework, on 763 fourth-grade students' preference for self-regulated learning, finding main ideas in expository texts and reading comprehension. The three conditions were regular classroom instruction (12 classes), students taught text reduction strategies (12 classes) and students who were taught text reduction strategies within the framework of a seven-step cyclical model of self-regulated learning (9 classes). At both post-test and 11-week follow-up, the TEXT + SRL students showed a stronger preference for self-regulated learning than others. They also identified more main ideas. Positive effects on reading comprehension in a standardized test were restricted to students without migration background.

García et al. (2016) analyzed differences in metacognitive skills between two groups of students (10–12 years) with different levels of metacognitive knowledge (high n = 50, low n = 64). Groups were based on students' scores on a test of knowledge of strategy use. Students reported the frequency with which they applied strategies during the phases of planning, execution and evaluation of learning. Results indicated that the group with high levels of metacognitive knowledge reported using their metacognitive skills significantly more frequently than peers.

A study of academic procrastination aimed to explore its relation with metacognitive self-regulation, self-efficacy and effort regulation (Ziegler & Opdenakker, 2018) with 566 students in 20 grade 1 secondary classes). SRL was negatively associated with procrastination, but diminishing over time, with effort regulation revealing the strongest association.

Gurcay and Ferah (2018) examined the relationships between 162 ninth-grade students' metacognitive self-regulation skills and physics self-efficacy beliefs and their critical thinking. The Critical Thinking Scale, Metacognitive Self-Regulation Scale and Physics Self-Efficacy Scale were measures. The students' metacognitive self-regulation and physics self-efficacy belief scores were significant predictors of their critical thinking scores, explaining 55% of the variance. The main variable that best explained critical thinking was metacognitive self-regulation, explaining 53% of the variance.

Schuster et al. (2020) investigated transfer of metacognitive skills in 233 fifth-grade children, asking whether students transfer metacognitive skills spontaneously and how to support metacognitive skill transfer. Participants were randomly assigned to six different conditions: two hybrid training conditions (metacognitive skills and one out of two cognitive strategies), two non-hybrid training conditions (only one out of two cognitive strategies) and two control training conditions (neither metacognitive skills nor cognitive strategies). After 15 weeks of training, transfer of metacognitive skills to learning tasks similar to training tasks (near transfer) was tested. In the following 15 weeks, all students received a second, non-hybrid, training involving a new cognitive strategy. Far transfer of metacognitive skills to the new cognitive strategy was tested afterward. The results showed that hybrid training, compared to non-hybrid and control training, improved both students' near and far transfer of metacognitive skills. Moreover, cognitive strategy use increased in at least one of the hybrid training conditions.

Assessment of Self-Regulated Learning

Now we turn to studies investigating the measurement of self-regulation skills, of which there are a number. We have already commented on Panadero (2017) and Prather et al. (2020) above, who gave useful information on measurement.

One can distinguish between instruments that measure SRL as an aptitude (including self-reporting questionnaires, structured interviews and teacher judgments) and those that measure it as an activity (think-aloud protocols, error detection in tasks, trace methodologies and observation) (Montalvo & Torres, 2004). In terms of measuring aptitude, self-reporting questionnaires included: the Learning and Study Strategies Inventory, the Motivated Strategies for Learning Questionnaire and the Components of Self-Regulated Learning. In terms of structured interviews, there was the Self-Regulated Learning Interview Schedule. Regarding teacher judgments, there was Rating Student Self-Regulated Learning Outcomes: A Teacher Scale. In terms of measuring activity, think-aloud protocols had been reported in reading and an answer protocol to assess student verbal response. There was no instrument for error detection, as this required the teacher to introduce errors into the relevant curriculum material. Trace methodologies were based on observable indicators regarding SRL processes that students deploy. Observations were based on judgments made by observers on what students do when they perform the tasks.

Conesa and Duñabeitia (2022) offered a Spanish version of the Academic Self-Regulation Questionnaire (SRQ-A), one of the most widely used instruments worldwide to measure academic motivation. Studying 1343 elementary school students aged 8–13 years, good convergent and discriminant validity of the Spanish version of the SRQ-A was shown.

Current pedagogical agents follow pre-established production rules based on temporal and frequency inputs from the learner, which limits the ability for these agents to provide individualized scaffolding intelligently and adaptively (Dever et al., 2022). This study introduces recurrence plots, which visualize system dynamics, as a novel method for enhancing learner models to provide pedagogical agents with the information necessary to interpret the dynamics of learners' enacted SRL processes. Learner models can be enhanced with information regarding learners' dynamic use of SRL processes to augment the accuracy and sophistication of pedagogical agent scaffolding.

Cleary and Russo (2023) provide a conceptual and empirical overview of a multimethod SRL diagnostic assessment framework included as part of the Self-Regulation Empowerment Program (SREP). Information about the operation and sequence of the SREP diagnostic assessment process is provided. The commonly used measures of SRL (e.g., self-report questionnaires, teacher rating scales, SRL microanalysis, think-aloud protocols) are analyzed and evidence provided supporting their psychometric rigor and utility in school settings. There was also a roadmap that could be used to increase the frequency and quality of school-based SRL assessments.

Few studies have examined whether survey items in questionnaires, verbal protocols and metacognitive judgments assess the same metacognitive skills or are related to the same learning outcomes (Zepeda & Nokes-Malach, 2023). The relations between three metacognitive regulation measures given at various points during a learning activity were investigated. Verbal protocols were collected during the learning activity, questionnaire responses were collected after the learning tasks but before the test, and judgments of knowing (JOKs) were collected during the test. Each measure was related to some aspect of performance, but the particular metacognitive skill, the direction of the effect and the type of learning outcome differed across the measures. These results highlight the heterogeneity of outcomes across the measures.

Zhang and Li (2023) reported on the development and validation of the Classroom Assessment for Self-Regulated Learning Questionnaire (CASRLQ), intended to measure to what extent assessment practices were SRL-supportive. The original CASRLQ, with 32 items representing five SRL-supportive CA dimensions, was administered to 469 grade 11 students. However, the preconceived structure was not supported. The authors then explored and verified a new factor structure employing exploratory and confirmatory factor analyses. A new sample of 630 grade 11 students were surveyed. The final form consisted of 28 items and addressed seven features: assessment tasks, student choice, self-assessment, peer assessment, instruction, teacher feedback and assessment environment. CASRLQ proved to be a reasonably reliable and valid instrument.

Specimen Program

Lee et al. (2023) aimed to investigate the effectiveness of self-regulated learning interventions led by teachers and applicable to three primary subjects (writing, mathematics, reading). There were three intervention studies (nStudy1 = 70, nStudy2 = 69, nStudy3 = 75). Trained teachers implemented the interventions – incorporating explicit instructions about domain-specific strategies in writing (Study 1), mathematics (Study 2), and reading (Study 3). Participants were assigned to one of the three groups: regular classroom instruction, domain-specific strategy instruction, and strategy instruction within the framework of eight-phase SRL instruction. Results revealed that the combined intervention group used more self-regulated strategies, performed better in achievement tests and were less distracted by task-irrelevant thoughts. These interventions were compatible with domain-specific instructions in multiple subjects and could guide and prompt self-regulatory learning processes in elementary classrooms.

Implementation

Teacher-led self-regulated learning interventions were developed applicable to three primary subjects – writing (Study 1), mathematics (Study 2) and reading (Study 3) – in authentic elementary school classrooms. The effects of self-regulated learning interventions on elementary school students' motivation and performance were examined in comparison with two other groups: (1) alternative intervention groups, who were taught domain-specific strategies only without instruction regarding self-regulated learning; and (2) no-treatment groups, who were exposed to regular classroom instructions.

A simplified version of Zimmerman's cyclical model was adopted, emphasizing cognitive and metacognitive aspects rather than the motivational aspect. It comprised seven steps: (1) self-assessment, (2) goal-setting, (3) strategic planning, (4) strategy implementation, (5) strategy monitoring, (6) strategy adjustment, and (7) outcome evaluation. The first three steps correspond to the forethought phase, in which students practiced setting optimal goals based on their self-assessment of their current competence. Then, they were guided to plan strategies to narrow the gap between the set goal and their current level of competence. The subsequent three steps corresponded to the performance phase. While implementing the planned strategies, students continued monitoring and adjusting their strategy use. The last step corresponded to the self-reflection phase. Students evaluated and reflected on their outcomes in comparison with the goals and strategies set at the beginning. Finally, an eight-phase cyclical model of self-regulated learning including self-assessment, task-analysis, goal-setting, strategic planning, strategy implementation, strategy monitoring, strategy adjustment and self-reflection was developed and implemented.

Classroom interventions should ideally be designed and implemented by teachers, because teachers are the most knowledgeable about their students and well-positioned to freely adjust details of interventions to their classroom contexts in an ecologically valid manner. Teachers can apply the cyclical model of SRL to diverse subject matters and customize it to their students with domain-specific strategies. Nonetheless, research has consistently reported that teacher-led self-regulated learning interventions show weaker effect sizes than research-led interventions. Furthermore, teachers tend to believe that self-regulated learning is challenging to teach and, therefore, do not feel confident that they can teach it. This implies that teachers implementing SRL interventions should be trained and taught about SRL in advance.

Teachers may encounter a range of obstacles during the implementation process in their classrooms. Teachers who underwent extensive workshops on strategy instruction seldom applied this instruction in their classrooms owing to: (1) setting factors (e.g., lack of administrative support and high start-up costs), (2) teacher factors (e.g., a poor mindset and failure to use critical teaching skills), (3) programmatic factors (e.g., lack of overall plans that specify how strategy instruction will be incorporated into ongoing instruction), and (4) instructional factors (e.g., high rates of interruptions during strategy instruction, bogging down during the instructional processes and not ensuring that students demonstrate mastery and generalization of the strategy).

During this study, teachers were provided one-on-one mentoring sessions with a research team member who explained and discussed what SRL was and how to teach it to elementary school students in classroom contexts. Communication channels (e.g., messengers, phone calls) were open with teachers during implementation to encourage them to discuss unexpected events or conflicts that might impede sessions. Furthermore, specific guidelines were followed to maximize the effects of SRL: Teachers provided explicit instructions, modeling and feedback regarding self-regulatory processes and strategy uses in the context of reading/writing or mathematics. Teachers explicitly explained what SRL is and why it was necessary, demonstrated instilling the self-regulatory processes and strategy uses and provided verbal feedback about students' SRL.

The authors designed and implemented pre-post quasi-experiments to examine group differences in self-regulated strategy use, task-irrelevant thoughts, self-efficacy and performance in subject domains, while controlling for the baseline scores. The teacher workshop was incorporated into a personalized one-on-one mentoring program for professional development. This program was conducted weekly for a month, with the flexibility to accommodate the schedules of each teacher. One of the researchers explained how to implement the Strategy plus SRL program in classes, with specific lesson plans and student worksheets. The teachers asked questions and rehearsed the program as if implementing it with the students. Then the teachers practiced and rehearsed the key instructions regarding introducing SRL in a particular domain. Five misunderstandings about SRL were re-introduced and all the teachers strongly disagreed with them.

The program contents for the Strategy (S) and Strategy + SRL (SRL) groups are given below in relation to each subject domain: writing, mathematics and reading.

Study 1 Writing

> Sessions 1–3: S had regular instruction while SRL had teacher instruction about SRL – what is SRL and why is it important, what are the eight phases of SRL, how can we use the eight-phase SRL model for writing an essay, how do the eight phases circulate and interact with each other?
>
> Sessions 4–5: For both S and SRL: Practice strategies: Teacher instruction about three writing strategies and practice of these in a short writing exercise, brainstorming, drawing a mind map, having a conversation about the topic with friends.
>
> Sessions 6–7: For both S and SRL: Teacher instruction in how to write a persuasive essay – what is a persuasive essay and why is it necessary, what are the main features of a persuasive essay, what is the format and composition of a persuasive essay?
>
> Sessions 8–12: For S: Writing practice: write a persuasive essay using the three writing strategies. For SRL: Writing practice: write a persuasive essay using the three writing strategies and eight phases of SRL as a whole process, teacher feedback about student SRL.

In Session 1, the teachers started by giving daily life examples requiring self-regulation, such as when students should resist the temptation to watch YouTube videos or play computer games instead of participating in online classes during COVID-19. Once students understood the examples, the teacher asked them to think and talk about scenarios wherein they failed to regulate themselves while studying. Based on the students' scenarios, the teachers emphasized the importance of self-regulated learning and highlighted the fact that several students did not know how to regulate their learning by themselves. Thereafter, the teachers clarified what self-regulated learning is and why it is highly important.

In Session 2, the teachers provided detailed instruction about the specifics of eight-phase self-regulated learning in the writing domain using a worksheet developed by the researchers and teachers. The worksheet contained specific questions reminding the students of what each phase means in the writing context. More precisely, for the self-assessment phase, a question asked, "How confident are you about [subject domain] and why?" For the task analysis phase, a question asked, "What does the [subject domain] task require you to think about?" For the goal-setting phase, a question asked, "What is your goal in this [subject domain] task?" For the strategic planning phase, a question asked, "Which strategy are you going to use to [subject domain]?" For the strategy implementation phase, a reminder saying "Stick to the strategy you planned" was presented instead of a question. For the strategy monitoring phase, a question asked, "Do you think the [subject domain] strategy you planned was appropriate for the [subject domain] task?" For the strategy adjustment phase, a question asked, "If you think the strategy does not fit well in the task, why do you not change your strategy?" For the outcome evaluation phase, a question asked, "Do you think your [subject domain] is satisfactory and why? If you are not satisfied with your [subject domain], what would you like to revise in your next [subject domain]?"

In Session 3, the teacher explained the cyclical feature of eight-phase SRL with examples of hypothetical students who knew what self-regulated learning was but failed to use the eight-phase model and demonstrated poor outcomes. Additionally, the teachers modeled how to use the eight-phase model during the task on thinking aloud. For instance, the teacher chose the sample topic, "Do we need to use smartphones at school?" Thereafter, she spoke about how confidently she could write an essay about this topic – as the first self-assessment phase of self-regulated learning. She then showed that she tried to infer why this topic was argumentative and worth considering as the second task in the analysis phase. Once she finished this, she set a goal to convince readers to agree with the necessity of using smartphones at school and to search and investigate what students are curious about as the third phase, goal-setting. Then, she selected the "talking with friends" strategy to elaborate on her idea and listened to the other opinions regarding the topic as the fourth strategic planning phase. While directing questions regarding the topic to other classmates and recording what they said, she organized supporting evidence to refute the opposing opinion as the fifth strategy implementation phase. After talking with classmates, she wrote the central argumentative sentences and provided supporting evidence. While writing, she re-read her sentences to monitor her writing (i.e., the sixth strategy monitoring phase) and find logical flaws – such as irrelevant supporting evidence to the main idea – as the seventh strategy adjustment phase. Lastly, she evaluated her writing for coherence, grammatical errors and extent of supporting evidence as the outcome evaluation phase.

After being introduced to self-regulated learning, students were taught three writing strategies, including brainstorming, mind mapping and conversing about the topic with friends, in Sessions 4 and 5. Teachers introduced these strategies individually and had students practice them when writing their essays. While writing, students received a worksheet encouraging them to remember and apply the eight-phase SRL model in addition to the strategies. The worksheet comprised a simple figure summary of the eight-phase self-regulated learning principles and a space to practice brainstorming, mind mapping and/or talking with friends about strategies.

Students were instructed regarding the specifics of writing an essay during Sessions 6 and 7. The sessions covered logistics and know-how regarding writing a persuasive essay, including what persuasive essays are, why they are necessary, what their main features are, their format and how to compose one. While providing instructions, the teacher attempted to clarify the connection between three writing strategies and the eight-phase self-regulated learning model she taught in previous sessions.

Once all the instructions were delivered, students practiced their writing daily for 40 minutes using three writing strategies and the eight-phase self-regulated learning model in Sessions 8–12. Throughout the five sessions, students wrote a persuasive essay every day about the following topics: "Is studying very important in our lives?"; "Are smartphones beneficial to us?"; "Is Simcheong in the traditional fairy tale a devoted or a selfish daughter?"; "Is it okay to use internet terms in daily life?"; and "Are exams necessary for us?"

All writing topics were relevant to students' daily lives and potentially controversial to make students provide reasonable evidence to support their argument. Students received a worksheet to guide the eight-phase self-regulated learning and strategy uses. The left side of the worksheet visualized the eight-phase self-regulated learning with a hopscotch pattern and asked students to write their answers about each phase. The right side was empty to encourage students to use writing strategies freely. After each writing practice, the teacher gave verbal feedback on students' SRL (e.g., "Your goal was too vague to achieve in this writing task"; "You appeared to forget the cyclical feature of self-regulated learning") without commenting on the writing quality per se.

Seventy fifth graders (38 boys, 32 girls; mean age = 10.46) from three classrooms at a public elementary school participated in the study. Each class was randomly assigned to one of the three conditions: control (n = 23), S (n = 24) and SRL (n = 23). Three elementary school teachers rated students' writing performance on four dimensions: (1) presence of reasonable evidence (0 = no, 1 = yes), (2) consistency of writing (0 = inconsistent, 1 = consistent), (3) clear paragraph division (0 = no, 1 = yes), and (4) composition of introduction, body, and conclusion (0 = no, 1 = yes). The mean score of the four dimensions was used as a writing performance indicator. Inter-rater reliability among the three teachers was 0.89. Students in the SRL group increased their self-regulated strategy use, whereas those in the other groups did not. The SRL group also showed enhanced writing performance from pre- to post-test more steeply than the other groups. Task-irrelevant thoughts and self-efficacy showed no difference.

Study 2 Mathematics

In Study 2, an SRL intervention in mathematics focused on solving word problems. Three representative strategies were selected: drawing a diagram, making a table and finding a rule, which were known to be widely used in solving mathematics word problems. Mathematics instructions about problem-solving strategies for these and the cyclical model of self-regulated learning were integrated within each session across the intervention, rather than separating them from each other. Thus, problem-solving strategies were expected to be better absorbed in the self-regulatory processes.

> Session 1: For S: Strategy instruction: Introduction plus teacher instruction on drawing a diagram strategy. For SRL: As for S plus introduction to SRL, what is SRL and why is it important, what are the eight phases of SRL, how can we use eight-phase SRL for solving mathematics word problems?
> Session 2: For S: Strategy practice: Solving word problems using the draw a diagram strategy. For SRL: As for S plus memorizing and getting used to eight-phase SRL while solving word problems.
> Session 3: For S: Teacher instruction about making a table strategy. For SRL: As for S plus teacher instruction about how the eight phases circulate and interact with each other.
> Session 4: For S: Practice – solving word problems using the make a table strategy. For SRL: As for S, plus practice cyclical SRL while solving word problems, plus teacher feedback about SRL.
> Session 5: For S: Instruction and practice regarding finding a rule. For SRL: As for S, plus practice cyclical SRL while solving word problems, plus teacher feedback about SRL.
> Session 6: For S: Solve word problems using the three strategies. For SRL: As for S plus teacher feedback about SRL.

In Study 2, 69 fourth graders (37 boys, 32 girls; mean age = 9.78) from three classrooms at a public elementary school participated. Each class was randomly assigned to one of three conditions: control (n = 21), Strategy (S) (n = 22) and Strategy + SRL (SRL) (n =26).

The duration of both intervention programs was three weeks (Week 1: Sessions 1 & 2, Week 2: Sessions 3 & 4, Week 3: Sessions 5 & 6). Students' performance in mathematics word problems before and after the interventions was measured using 12 short-answer questions developed by the teachers. The difficulty level of the pre- and post-test problems was equivalent. Students in the SRL group increased their self-regulated strategy use, whereas those in the S and control groups did not. The SRL group showed reduced task-irrelevant thoughts in comparison with the control and S groups. The SRL group also had greatly enhanced mathematics performance compared to the other groups.

Study 3 Reading

The Think Before, While and After (TWA) reading strategy was selected, which had been widely used in elementary school children's reading comprehension. It consists of nine specific strategies, including thinking about "the author's purpose", "what you know", "what you want to know", "reading speed", "linking knowledge", "rereading parts", "the main idea", "summarizing information", and "what you learned". Examples and representative cases were distributed during the instruction and worksheets also referred to reading comprehension.

> Session 1: Strategy (S) and Strategy + Self-Regulated Learning (SRL) groups both had an introduction to the TWA strategy.
> Session 2: S read a news article using TWA; SRL had an introduction to SRL following the model for previous studies.
> Session 3: S read a discussion paper using TWA; SRL read a news article using TWA.
> Session 4: S read a story using TWA; SRL read a discussion paper using TWA and were introduced to the cyclical model of SRL – how the eight phases circulate and interact with each other.
> Session 5: S read a story using TWA; SRL did the same plus practice of cyclical SRL while reading the story.
> Session 6: S read an essay using TWA; SRL read a story using TWA plus practice of how to diagnose one's phase accurately and circulate phases.

Session 7: S read an expository text using TWA; SRL read an essay using TWA.

Session 8: S had regular class instruction; SRL read an expository text using TWA plus practiced SRL as a whole process while reading.

A total of 75 sixth graders (39 boys, 36 girls; mean age = 11.35) from three classes at a public elementary school participated in Study 3. Each class was randomly assigned to one of three conditions: control (n = 25), Strategy (S) (n = 25) or Strategy + SRL (SRL) (n = 25). The duration of the SRL intervention was four weeks (Week 1: Sessions 1 & 2, Week 2: Sessions 3 & 4, Week 3: Sessions 5–7, Week 4: Session 8), and that of the S intervention three weeks (Week 1: Sessions 1 & 2, Week 2: Sessions 3 & 4, Week 3: Sessions 5–7). Students' reading comprehension performance before and after the interventions was assessed using eight items which were combinations of multiple-choice and short-answer questions developed by the teachers. Self-efficacy and performance were higher for the SRL group than for the other groups, but the difference did not reach statistical significance. Nor was there a difference in self-regulated strategy use. Students in the SRL group showed a significantly steeper decrease in task-irrelevant thoughts than the control or Strategy groups.

Overall Findings

Considering all three studies together, comparing the SRL group to controls, the SRL group were better on self-regulated strategy use (ES = 0.50), task-irrelevant thoughts (ES = 1.00), self-efficacy (ES = 0.30) and performance (ES = 0.96). Comparing the SRL group to the Strategy group, the SRL group were better on self-regulated strategy use (ES = 0.79), task-irrelevant thoughts (ES = 0.82) and performance (ES = 0.94), but not significantly on self-efficacy (ES = 0.10). The Strategy group were only significantly better than controls on one variable (self-regulated strategy use).

References

Cleary, T. J., & Russo, M. R. (2023). A multilevel framework for assessing self-regulated learning in school contexts: Innovations, challenges, and future directions. *Psychology in the Schools*, 1–23. https://doi.org/10.1002/pits.23035

Conesa, P. J., & Duñabeitia, J. A. (2022). Adaptation and validation to Spanish elementary school children of the Academic Self-Regulation Questionnaire (SRQ-A). *Electronic Journal of Research in Educational Psychology*, *20*(2), 403–426. https://doi.org/10.25115/ejrep.v20i57.6013

de Boer, H., Donker-Bergstra, A. S., & Kostons, D. D. N. M. (2012). *Effective Strategies for Self-Regulated Learning: A Meta-Analysis*. Groningen: Gronings Instituut voor Onderzoek van Onderwijs, Rijksuniversiteit Groningen.

Dever, D., Wiedbusch, M., & Azevedo, R. (2022). Enhancing learner models for pedagogical agent scaffolding of self-regulated learning. In S. Iyer et al. (Eds.), *Proceedings of the 30th International Conference on Computers in Education*, Asia-Pacific Society for Computers in Education.

Dignath, C., & Büttner, G. (2008). Components of fostering self-regulated learning among students. A meta-analysis on intervention studies at primary and secondary school level. *Metacognition and Learning*, *3*, 231–264. doi: 10.1007/s11409-008-9029-x

Dignath, C., Büttner, G., & Langfeldt, H. (2008). How can primary school students learn self-regulated learning strategies most effectively? A meta-analysis on self-regulation training programmes. *Educational Research Review*, *3*(2), 101–129. doi: 10.1016/j.edurev.2008.02.003

Efklides, A., & Metallidou, P. (2020). Applying metacognition and self-regulated learning in the classroom. *Oxford Research Encyclopedia of Education*. https://doi.org/10.1093/acrefore/9780190264093.013.961

Elhusseini, S. S., Tischner, C. M., Aspiranti, K. B., & Fedewa, A. L. (2022). A quantitative review of the effects of self-regulation interventions on primary and secondary student academic achievement.

Metacognition and Learning, 17, 1117–1139. https://doi.org/10.1007/s11409-022-09311-0

García, T., Rodríguez, C., González-Castro, P., Álvarez-García, D., & González-Pienda, J.-A. (2016). Metacognition and executive functioning in elementary school. *Anales de Psicología, 32*(2), 474–483. http://dx.doi.org/10.6018/analesps.32.2.202891

Gurcay, D., & Ferah, H. O. (2018). High school students' critical thinking related to their metacognitive self-regulation and physics self-efficacy beliefs. *Journal of Education and Training Studies, 6*(4), 125–130. https://doi.org/10.11114/jets.v6i4.2980

Lee, M. H., Lee, S. Y., Kim, J. E., & Lee, H. J. (2023). Domain-specific self-regulated learning interventions for elementary school students. *Learning and Instruction, 88*, 101810. https://doi.org/10.1016/j.learninstruc.2023.101810

Loksa, D., Margulieux, L., Becker, B. A., Craig, M., Denny, P., Pettit, R., & Prather, J. (2022). Metacognition and self-regulation in programming education: Theories and exemplars of use. *ACM Transactions on Computing Education, 22*(4), Article 39. https://doi.org/10.1145/3487050

Montalvo, F. T., & Torres, M. C. G. (2004). Self-regulated learning: Current and future directions. *Electronic Journal of Research in Educational Psychology, 2*(1), 1–34.

Muir, R. A., Howard, S. J., & Kervin, L. (2023). Interventions and approaches targeting early self-regulation or executive functioning in preschools: A systematic review. *Educational Psychology Review, 35*(27), 1–32. https://doi.org/10.1007/s10648-023-09740-6

Panadero, E. (2017). A review of self-regulated learning: Six models and four directions for research. *Frontiers in Psychology, 8*(422). doi: 10.3389/fpsyg.2017.00422

Perkins, D. N., & Salomon, G. (1992). *Transfer of learning. International Encyclopedia of Education*, 2nd edition. Oxford: Pergamon Press.

Pintrich, P. R. (2000). The role of goal orientation in self-regulated learning. In M. Boekaerts, P. R. Pintrich, & M. Zeidner (Eds.), *Handbook of Self-Regulation* (pp. 451–502). San Diego: Academic Press.

Prather, J., Becker, B. A., Craig, M., Denny, P., Loksa, D., & Margulieux, L. (2020). What do we think we think we are doing? Metacognition and self-regulation in programming. *Learning Sciences Faculty Publications, 36*. https://doi.org/10.1145/3372782.3406263

Schuster, C., Stebner, F., Leutner, D., & Wirth, J. (2020). Transfer of metacognitive skills in self-regulated learning: An experimental training study. *Metacognition and Learning*, *15*, 455–477. https://doi.org/10.1007/s11409-020-09237-5

Sitzmann, T., & Ehly, K. (2011). A meta-analysis of self-regulated learning in work-related training and educational attainment: What we know and where we need to go. *Psychological Bulletin*, *137*(3), 421–442. doi: 10.1037/a0022777

Stoeger, H., Sontag, C., & Ziegler, A. (2014). Impact of a teacher-led intervention on preference for self-regulated learning, finding main ideas in expository texts, and reading comprehension. *Journal of Educational Psychology*, *106*(3), 799–814. doi: 10.1037/a0036035

Xu, Z. H., Zhao, Y. Y., Zhang, B. S., Liew, J., & Kogut, A. (2022). A meta-analysis of the efficacy of self-regulated learning interventions on academic achievement in online and blended environments in K-12 and higher education. *Behaviour & Information Technology*. https://doi.org/10.1080/0144929X.2022.2151935

Yu, B., & Zhang, G. Y. (2023). The effects of learning analytics on online self-regulated learning: A meta-analysis. In A. W. B. Tso, S. K. K. Ng, L. Law, & T. S. Bai (Eds.), *The Post-Pandemic Landscape of Education and Beyond: Innovation and Transformation*. HKAECT 2022. Educational Communications and Technology Yearbook. Singapore: Springer. https://doi.org/10.1007/978-981-19-9217-9_10

Zepeda, C. D., & Nokes-Malach, T. J. (2023). Assessing metacognitive regulation during problem solving: A comparison of three measures. *Journal of Intelligence*, *11*(16). https://doi.org/10.3390/jintelligence11010016

Zhang, W. X., & Li, Y. Q. (2023). Development and validation of a questionnaire to assess classroom assessment from the self-regulated learning perspective. *Oxford Review of Education*. https://doi.org/10.1080/03054985.2023.2174092

Ziegler, N., & Opdenakker, M. (2018). The development of academic procrastination in first-year secondary education students. *Learning and Individual Differences*, *64*, 71–82. doi: 10.1016/j.lindif.2018.04.009

Zimmerman, B. J., & Schunk, D. H. (2011). *Handbook of Self-Regulation of Learning and Performance*. New York: Routledge.

Section D

Programs Focusing Especially on Memory and Disability

17
Metacognition and Memory

While metacognition has components of knowledge and skill, it is also highly dependent on student motivation. But beyond this, metacognition also depends upon memory (or to be more precise, as psychologists like to say, "working memory", meaning how we temporarily remember information that we need in the moment, like recalling a phone number or recalling directions). It is fairly obvious that if you cannot keep the parts of a problem in your mind, you are going to have trouble solving the problem with any global or holistic strategy.

Definition

Working memory is the small amount of information that can be held in mind and used in the execution of cognitive tasks, in contrast with long-term memory, which is the vast amount of information saved in one's life. It is a cognitive system with a limited capacity that can hold information temporarily. It is not the same as short-term memory (which is just about storing information), since working memory implies that information is being held to be manipulated to solve some kind of problem.

Numerous models have been proposed for how working memory functions. Miller (1956) claimed that the working memory capacity of young adults was around seven elements, referred to as "chunks", but of course this would vary between people. Individual differences in working memory capacity are to some extent heritable; that is, about half of the variation between individuals is related to differences in their genes. A study of school-age children with significant learning disabilities showed that working memory capacity, but not IQ, predicted learning outcomes two years later (Alloway, 2009).

The amount of forgetting depends on the temporal density of attentional demands of the processing task – this density is called "cognitive load". Cognitive load depends on two other variables, the rate at which the processing task requires individual steps to be carried out and the duration of each step. Working memory is impaired by psychological stress.

Background

There are a few recent reviews of memory and metacognition. In Schneider's (2010) chapter, the focus is on the development of metamemory, which refers to children's awareness of their own memory performance. Two main metamemory categories have been proposed: "sensitivity" and "variables". The "sensitivity" category refers to mostly implicit, unconscious behavioral knowledge of when memory is necessary. The "variables" category refers to explicit, conscious and factual knowledge about the importance of person, task and strategy variables for memory performance.

Spencer-Smith and Klingberg (2015) meta-analyzed the effects of a working memory training program (specifically CogMed) on everyday life. Twelve studies were located and the meta-analysis showed a significant positive training effect on inattention in daily life (ES = 0.47). This was true for both visuospatial and verbal tasks. Significant effects were observed in both children and adults, and in users with and without ADHD (Attention Deficit Hyperactivity Disorder). Seven of the studies reported follow-up assessment showing persisting training benefits (ES = 0.33).

A specific focus on typically developing children characterized the meta-analysis of Sala and Gobet (2017), which included

26 studies and 1601 children aged 3–16 years. It focused on the effects of working memory training on cognitive and academic skills (e.g., fluid intelligence, attention/inhibition, mathematics and literacy). The authors noted that the idea that far transfer may take place in working memory training was still controversial. They found that whereas working memory training exerted a significant effect on short-term cognitive skills (ES = 0.46), little evidence was found regarding far-transfer effects (ES = 0.12). Moreover, the size of the effects was inversely related to the quality of the design (i.e., random allocation to the groups and presence of an active control group).

Turning to individual studies, Autin and Croizet (2012) conducted three randomized experiments (n = 310) to test the effectiveness of an intervention to boost working memory. Sixth graders either received or did not receive a ten-minute intervention designed to reframe metacognitive interpretation of difficulty as indicative of learning rather than of self-limitation. The intervention improved children's working memory span and reading comprehension and also reduced thoughts of incompetence.

The effects of working memory capacity on students' mathematical problem solving were explored by Alikamar et al. (2013). Female high school students (n = 256) aged 17–18 were tested on: (a) Metacognitive Awareness Inventory, (b) Mathematics Attention Test, (c) Mathematics Anxiety Rating Scale, (d) Digit Span Backward Test, and (e) a mathematics test. In every comparison of low/high metacognition, low/high mathematics attention and low/high mathematics anxiety, the students with high working memory capacity showed better mathematical performance than students with low capacity.

Rode et al. (2014) tested the effectiveness of an intensive 17-session adaptive computerized working memory training program for improving performance on paper and pencil working memory tasks, standardized school achievement tasks and teacher ratings of classroom behavior. Third-grade children either received the computerized working memory training for about 30 minutes per session (n = 156) or participated in regular classroom activities (n = 126). Pre-test and post-test transfer measures of working memory and school achievement, as well as teacher ratings, showed substantial correlations with training task performance. However, effect sizes of transfer gains were small and inconsistent across tasks.

Cornoldi et al. (2015) examined the feasibility of improving problem-solving skills in school children by means of a training program that addressed general and specific abilities involved in problem solving, focusing on metacognition and working memory. Participants were 135 primary school children attending eight classes in the third, fourth and fifth grades (age range 8–10 years). The classes were assigned to two groups, intervention and control. The training program led to improvements in both metacognitive and working memory tasks, with positive effects on the ability to solve problems. The gains were maintained at follow-up after three months.

Bozorgian et al. (2020) investigated the effect of a ten-session metacognitive intervention on the listening performance and metacognitive awareness of 136 male learners of English as a Foreign Language with low working memory capacity. Sixty learners with low working memory were randomly assigned to experimental (n = 30) and control (n = 30) groups. Listening tests were completed before and after the intervention. The intervention group had a higher gain, with a moderate effect size in terms of listening performance, than the control group.

Specimen Program

Jones et al. (2020) noted that working memory training had been shown to improve performance on new working memory tasks in typically developing children, but there was limited evidence that it improved academic outcomes. The lack of transfer to academic outcomes might have been because children were only learning skills and strategies in a very narrow context, which they were unable to apply to other tasks. Metacognitive strategy interventions, which promote metacognitive awareness and teach children general strategies that can be used on a variety of tasks, might be needed to bridge the gap between specific memories and wider application, i.e., to promote transfer.

Ninety-five typically developing children aged 9–14 years were randomly allocated to three cognitive training programs that were conducted daily after school. One group received "Cogmed" working memory training (Klingberg et al., 2005), another group received concurrent Cogmed and metacognitive strategy training, and the control group received adaptive visual search training.

Children were assessed on four working memory tasks, reading comprehension and mathematical reasoning, before, immediately after and three months after training. Working memory training improved working memory and mathematical reasoning relative to the control group. These improvements in working memory were maintained three months later and they were significantly greater for the group that received metacognitive strategy training compared to working memory training alone. Working memory training seemed a potentially effective educational intervention when provided in conjunction with metacognition training and in addition to school. Future research would need to investigate ways to maintain academic improvements long term and to optimize metacognitive strategy training to promote far transfer.

Implementation

This study used a "Cognitive Training Workbook" which is available at https://osf.io/7dh93. The structure of the workbook is given below. As this is readily available online, further details will not be given here, except for the contents.

Session 0 Using This Workbook
Session 1 MAI Questionnaire
Session 2 Introduction
Session 3 Reflecting on Memory
Session 4 Reflecting on Reading Comprehension
Session 5 Reflecting on Mathematics Problem Solving
Session 6 Want to Think Metacognitively? Then PME!
Session 7 Strategize with Strategies!

Session 8 Personal Strategy Guide
Session 9 Mind-Set Strategies
Session 10 PME in Practice – Memory 1
Session 11 PME in Practice – Reading Comprehension 1
Session 12 PME in Practice – Mathematics Problem Solving 1
Session 13 PME in Practice – Memory 2
Session 14 PME in Practice – Reading Comprehension 2
Session 15 PME in Practice – Mathematics Problem Solving 2
Session 16 PME in Practice – Memory 3
Session 17 PME in Practice – Reading Comprehension 3
Session 18 PME in Practice – Mathematics Problem Solving 3
Session 19 PME in Practice – Memory 4
Session 20 PME in Practice – Reading Comprehension 4
Session 21 PME in Practice – Mathematics Problem Solving 4
Session 22 PME in Practice – Memory 5
Session 23 PME in Practice – Reading Comprehension 5
Session 24 PME in Practice – Mathematics Problem Solving 5
Session 25 MAI Questionnaire

References

Alikamar, M. A., Alamolhodaei, H., & Radmehr, F. (2013). The role of metacognition on effect of working memory capacity on students' mathematical problem solving. *European Journal of Child Development, Education and Psychopathology*, *1*(3), 125–139.

Alloway, T. P. (2009). Working memory, but not IQ, predicts subsequent learning in children with learning difficulties. *European Journal of Psychological Assessment*, *25*(2), 92–98. doi: 10.1027/1015-5759.25.2.92

Autin, F., & Croizet, J.-C. (2012). Improving working memory efficiency by reframing metacognitive interpretation of task difficulty. *Journal of Experimental Psychology: General*, *141*(4), 610–661. doi: 10.1037/a0027478

Bozorgian, H., Yaqubi, B., & Muhammadpour, M. (2020). Metacognitive intervention and awareness: Listeners with low working memory capacity. *International Journal of Listening*, doi: 10.1080/10904018.2020.1857764

Cornoldi, C., Carretti, B., Drusi, S., & Tencat, C. (2015). Improving problem solving in primary school students: The effect of a training programme focusing on metacognition and working memory. *British Journal of Educational Psychology*, *85*, 424–439. doi: 10.1111/bjep.12083

Jones, J. S., Milton, F., Mostazir, M., & Adlam, A. R. (2020). The academic outcomes of working memory and metacognitive strategy training in children: A double-blind randomized controlled trial. *Developmental Science*, *23*, e12870. doi: 10.1111/desc.12870

Klingberg, T., Fernell, E., Olesen, P. J., Johnson, M., Gustafsson, P., Dahlström, K., … Westerberg, H. (2005). Computerized training of working memory in children with ADHD – A randomized, controlled trial. *Journal of the American Academy of Child & Adolescent Psychiatry*, *44*, 177–186. https://doi.org/10.1097/00004583-20050 2000-00010

Miller, G. A. (1956). The magical number seven plus or minus two: Some limits on our capacity for processing information. *Psychological Review*, *63*(2), 81–97. doi: 10.1037/h0043158

Rode, C., Robson, R., Purviance, A., Geary, D. C., & Mayr, U. (2014). Is working memory training effective? A study in a school setting. *PLoS ONE*, *9*(8), e104796. doi: 10.1371/journal.pone.0104796

Sala, G., & Gobet, F. (2017). Working memory training in typically developing children: A meta-analysis of the available evidence. *Developmental Psychology*, *53*, 671–685. https://doi.org/10.1037/dev0000265

Schneider, W. (2010). Metacognition and memory development in childhood and adolescence. In H. Salatas Waters and W. Schneider (Eds.), *Metacognition, Strategy Use and Instruction*. New York. Guilford Press.

Spencer-Smith, M., & Klingberg, T. (2015). Benefits of a working memory training program for inattention in daily life: A systematic review and meta-analysis. *PLoS ONE*, *10*, e0119522. https://doi.org/10.1371/journal.pone.0119522

18

Metacognition, Memory and Disability

Students with disabilities or special needs (especially those with Learning Difficulties or Attention Deficit Hyperactivity Disorder – ADHD) might struggle more with memory in general (and working memory in particular) than regular students. Consequently, given that metacognition is to an extent dependent on memory, attempts to enhance their metacognitive abilities might need to take this into account and try to enhance working memory as well as metacognition. Working memory is the limited amount of information that can temporarily be held in mind to be manipulated to solve some kind of problem.

Definition

The definition of working memory in Chapter 17 applies here also: It is the limited amount of information that can temporarily be held in mind to be used in the execution of cognitive tasks. Working memory implies that information is being held to be manipulated to solve some kind of problem.

Learning Difficulties or Disabilities is a category of special educational need. Someone with a learning disability has a significantly reduced ability to understand new or complex information or skills. They may learn in a different way or need information presented to them in lots of different ways. This might be associated with a reduced ability to cope with life independently – things like managing money or socializing. Learning difficulties can vary from mild through moderate to severe. Learning disabilities are lifelong conditions. Learning disability is different for everyone – no two people with a learning disability are the same.

Attention Deficit and Hyperactivity Disorder (ADHD) is also a category of special educational need, with symptoms including inattention (not being able to keep focus or concentrate), hyperactivity (restless with excess movement such as fidgeting that is not appropriate to the setting) and impulsivity (hasty acts that occur in the moment without thought).

So far as metacognition is concerned, for the person with ADHD memory is affected at the input stage as the person cannot sustain attention, while for a person with learning difficulty memory is more affected at the processing stage.

Background

Learning Difficulties

There is a meta-analysis of metacognition in students with learning disabilities (Maxwell & Grenier, 2014), which explores previous research involving metacognitive interventions and the academic performance of students with learning disabilities. From an initial review of 120 studies, only six studies met the inclusion criteria. A medium-to-large effect size of 0.79 was found, although all measures were non-standardized. Thus, metacognitive treatments for students with learning disabilities throughout elementary to post-secondary settings seemed effective.

Turning to individual studies, the effects of computer-based working memory training were explored by Partanen et al. (2015) using two training procedures with 64 children with learning disabilities from ten primary schools. The children were randomized into either a working memory training group or a working memory plus metacognitive strategy training group.

Measures of general cognitive ability, auditory and visuospatial working memory, arithmetic ability, and reading and writing skills were gathered. Results showed a significant difference in working memory performance in favor of the metacognitive intervention. Furthermore, transfer effects occurred on working memory measures at six-month follow-up. However, there was no transfer to academic achievement.

The ability to use metacognitive strategies for reading and the phonological working memory of school children with learning disabilities was investigated by Nicolielo-Carrilho et al. (2018). Thirty school-age children aged 8–12 years of both genders were divided into two groups, experimental and control. Measures were evaluation of reading comprehension, phonological working memory and use of metacognitive skills for reading. The intervention group was significantly different from the control group. Reading comprehension, phonological working memory and metacognitive tests were significantly correlated.

A quasi-experimental study with pre-test and post-test and control group was undertaken by Zolfy et al. (2022), who investigated the effect of teaching metacognitive strategies on working memory and response inhibition. Thirty students with specific learning disabilities in reading were selected and randomly assigned to experimental and control groups. Measures were Wechsler 4, Stroop, N-Beck's Working Memory and a checklist. The Cognitive-Metacognitive Strategy Training Program was used. The experimental group received the program in 18 sessions of 45 minutes. There was a very significant difference between experimental and control groups. Training of cognitive-metacognitive strategies improved working memory scores and response inhibition.

Attention Deficit and Hyperactivity Disorder (ADHD)

Pisacco et al. (2018) compared the effects of two metacognitive interventions on writing, working memory and behavioral symptoms of students with ADHD. The first approach was a combined intervention in text production and working memory, while the second focused only on working memory. Participants were 47 students from the fifth to ninth grades of two public elementary schools, randomized to one of the two intervention groups. Writing and working memory were assessed before, immediately after and three months after the interventions. Both interventions contributed to improving behavior and school performance, but only the combined intervention increased the overall quality of narrative text, organization of paragraphs and denouement.

The aim of another study (Capodieci et al., 2019) was to devise a training that combined individual exercises on visuospatial working memory and group metacognitive activities which might help children with ADHD to ameliorate their performance in executive functioning tasks, and to contain their inattentive and hyperactive/impulsive behavior. It was administered to 12 children with ADHD and 15 typically-developing children. Tasks on executive functions and questionnaires for parents and teachers were administered before and at the end of the training and one month after the post-test. Specific gains and transfer effects were found at the post-test and follow-up assessments in both typically-developing children and those with ADHD. Parents' and teachers' ratings also indicated an improvement in the symptomatic behavior of children with ADHD. Thus, a training that combined working memory activities with metacognitive group reflection about useful strategies produced promising results.

A study to check whether memory would be strengthened by three months of metacognitive training using mnemonic techniques (Mind Maps and SketchNoting) in children with ADHD was conducted by Kajka (2019). Forty-five 10-year-old children took part, randomly assigned to the Mind Map group, the SketchNoting group or a control group. All groups took the Deferred Naming Test before and after the training. Working memory improved in all groups, but the error count was lowest in the Mind Map group and highest in the control group. Thus, Mind Maps can be an important tool to strengthen memory for children with ADHD.

Specimen Program

Domain-specific working memory deficits are encountered in children with mathematics learning difficulties. David and

Maier (2011) investigated the effectiveness of two different types of training on the mathematical performance of low achieving students. A training of working memory and a training of metacognitive skills were selected, as applied to mathematics. It seemed reasonable to consider a program based on metacognition, as many mathematical activities are approached in a systematic and algorithmic manner.

Both programs were efficient in enhancing operational fluency in simple and complex mathematics problems, with no difference between them. These results could be used to add to the behavioral profile of children with mathematics learning disabilities.

Implementation

The hypothesis was that if the students with moderate learning difficulty showed lower attention control, then training this function in specific mathematical situations would improve performance in arithmetical problems, where arithmetical facts were not automatic and therefore an active manipulation with numerical material was needed, together with a temporary storage of partial results and intermediate steps. Previous studies mostly investigated the effects of metacognitive training on performance in word problems and not in arithmetical problems, although these also involved planning, steps monitoring and estimation of task difficulty.

Participants were 72 third graders from three classes in one school. Based on pre-test results, participants with low scores were selected and assigned to three groups, of which two had further training and one was the control group. Each group consisted of an equal number of students from each class, in order to avoid any influences of teaching style. One week before the training, participants were tested with a calculation fluency task, a working memory task and a metacognitive instrument. One week after the training, post-test measures were administered.

Both trainings were conducted over a three-week period, with two weekly sessions of 50 minutes each. Sessions were conducted in small groups of four to five children to facilitate group discussions and to reduce the demands of the working memory group tasks. All sessions were conducted in school, in the resource room apart from their classrooms.

The metacognitive training was created to improve the metacognitive knowledge and metacognitive strategies of students with low performance in mathematics. The first training session was introductory and consisted of a short presentation of the training and the four stages: the modeling stage, the practice stage with teacher's support, the cooperation stage and the individual practice stage. In the second session the importance of metacognitive questions in each of the stages was discussed. Semantically similar questions were formulated by the group and written down on colored cards (What do we know and what do we need to find out? What is the given data? What strategies are more appropriate to solve this arithmetical problem? What is similar to/different from other problems solved before? Am I able to solve it independently? What were the difficulties that I encountered when solving the problem? How can I check the answer? Is there another way to solve it? Which one is the more efficient way to solve it?).

In the third session the first two stages were discussed: the modeling stage and the practice stage with teacher's help; their importance, the way of developing the stage when working on a specific arithmetical problem. In the fourth session the other two stages were discussed: the cooperation stage and the individual practice stage. During the fifth session, students practiced this model on different arithmetical problems. The last meeting consisted of emphasizing the importance of this model and the way it could influence school performance.

The domain-specific working memory training addressed the enhancement of working memory abilities specifically in the numerical domain and contained not only numerical material, but also numerical processing. All activities were designed in order to contain concomitantly temporary storage of numerical information and processing. All training sessions were presented as games for motivational purposes.

In the first session, children played a numbers game which consisted of filling in an incomplete number chart with numbers from 0 to 100. Each child received only a fourth of the chart to complete. After completion, they were asked to recall the numbers they wrote. In the calculation game, they were asked to solve multi-digit vertical additions. After completion, they were asked to recall the numerical material. The calculation results were not corrected.

In the second session, a well-known working memory task (counting span) was used and adapted to be applicable simultaneously to groups of four children. Children were given cards with dots. Dots were green and yellow on a blue background and were randomly distributed on the card. Dots were the same size. The set size varied from six yellow dots to 14. The task consisted of counting the yellow dots and recalling the order of presentation of all the counted amounts on four cards. The processing task was to decide who had the card with the greatest number of dots in each counting trial. The child with the greatest number had to raise his/her hand to signal it.

In the "one meter of numbers" game, children were given numbers from zero to nine written in words in a single row on a long paper strip (seven to eight number words). They had to read them silently, memorize them and add up the last two. When recalling the numbers, a piece from the strip was cut containing the numbers recalled correctly. At the end, all the pieces were put together and measured to see if the group had managed to add up to a meter of strip.

In session three, three activities were included. In the "where does the phone ring" game, children received small cards with phone numbers of six to seven digits with the first three digits identical and in the same order while the last four digits were randomized. Children had to memorize the digits in the given sequence and add up the last two. Afterwards, the trainer "dialed" a phone number and the children had to recognize the number and say "ring ring".

The "Sudoku numbers" game required the children to fill in Sudoku charts with numbers from one to four. On a small card there were four Sudoku squares assigned to four children (each child had one square to fill in). The rules were explained and a trial session was run. Children were given a few seconds to identify the missing numbers according to the Sudoku rules. Each child had to name and ask for the two missing numbers on his/her square after the square was removed.

The "geographical superlatives" game was presented as a general knowledge contest. Children had to listen to a statement with geographical superlatives and numerical information. Afterwards, they were asked a processing question referring to other information from the same statement. After answering the question children were asked to recall the number.

In session four, the "chain addition" game was played. The children were sitting in a circle. A starting point (a random number) was established by the teacher. The first child had to add six to the given number. The second had to add six to the sum obtained by the first one and so on. When someone gave a wrong answer, the child received a penalty card that stopped him/her for the next trial. The game continued until all children had difficulties with the addition.

In session five, the classical game of "the orange" was played. The children had to roll a pair of dice and had to remember the numbers obtained. The teacher started the game by saying "I would like to eat (e.g. 4) … oranges". The child that recognized his/her number answered "Why 4 and not e.g. 6?" The child recognizing the number six would do the same by choosing a different number. In "alternative addition", children were supposed to make a chain addition (the same as the previous game described in session four), but this time adding alternatively number six and number five. The same rules were applied.

References

Capodieci, A., Re, A. M., Fracca, A., Borella, E., & Carretti, B. (2019). The efficacy of a training that combines activities on working memory and metacognition: Transfer and maintenance effects in children with ADHD and typical development. *Journal of Clinical and Experimental Neuropsychology, 41*(10), 1074–1087. https://doi.org/10.1080/13803395.2019.1651827

David, C., & Maier, A. (2011). The effects of working memory training vs. metacognitive training on math performance of low achieving students. *Studia Universitatis Babes-Bolyai – Psychologia-Paedagogia*, *56*(1), 89–100.

Kajka, N. (2019). The influence of metacognitive training on the improvement of working memory in children with ADHD. *Current Problems in Psychiatry*, *20*(3), 217–227. doi: 10.2478/cpp-2019-0015

Maxwell, B. R., & Grenier, K. (2014). The effects of metacognitive treatments on the academic performance of students with learning disabilities: A meta-analysis. *Canadian Journal for New Scholars in Education*, *5*(1), 1–17.

Nicolielo-Carrilho, A. P., Crenitte, P. A. P., Lopes-Herrera, S. A., & Hage, S. R. D. (2018). Relationship between phonological working memory, metacognitive skills and reading comprehension in children with learning disabilities. *Journal of Applied Oral Science*, *26*, e20170414. http://dx.doi.org/10.1590/1678-7757-2017-0414

Partanen, P., Jansson, B., Lisspers, J., & Sundin, Ö. (2015). Metacognitive strategy training adds to the effects of working memory training in children with special educational needs. *International Journal of Psychological Studies*, *7*(3), 130–140. http://dx.doi.org/10.5539/ijps.v7n3p130

Pisacco, N. M. T., Sperafico, Y. L. S., Enricone, J. R. B., Guimarães, L. S. P., Rohde, L. A., & Dorneles, B. V. (2018). Metacognitive interventions in text production and working memory in students with ADHD. *Psicologia: Reflexão e Crítica*, *31*(5). doi: 10.1186/s41155-017-0081-9

Zolfy, V., Hosseini-Nasab, S. D., & Azmoudeh, M. (2022). The effect of teaching cognitive-metacognitive strategies on working memory and response inhibition of students with special learning disorders such as reading. *Journal of Learning Disabilities*, *11*(2), 62–76. https://doi.org/10.22098/jld.2022.7366.1789

Section E

Programs Embedded in Digital Technology

19

Computerized and Online Learning

There are two kinds of interventions considered here. By "computerized interventions" we mean learning materials which are located on computers and can be accessed on computers in schools. By "online interventions" we mean learning materials which are delivered through the internet and can be accessed in any place (and often at any time).

Definition

Computerized intervention or computer-based learning (CBL) makes use of the interactive elements of computer hardware and computer applications and software. It has the ability to present many kinds of media to users – text, pictures, graphics, audio, video, hypermedia, and so on. Computer-based learning has many benefits, including the advantage of users learning at their own pace and learning without the need for an instructor to be physically present. It is essentially "offline" (i.e., not connected to the internet, although it may be connected to a local area network).

Online interventions are learning materials and experiences available on or performed by using a connection to the internet or other computer network, through a computer, tablet or mobile phone. They have the advantages of computer-based learning and in addition can be accessed anywhere (there is an internet connection) and at any time.

Research has focused on many aspects of CBL, such as the role of pedagogical agents, reflection prompts, embedded scaffolds, navigation support, expert modeling, system structure, comprehension aids, and fixed and adaptive scaffolds. In general, student learning of challenging material can be enhanced by adaptive scaffolding (rather than fixed) that addresses both domain content and self-regulated learning.

Background

There are several reviews of research in this area. An early review by Winters et al. (2008) selected 33 empirical studies of self-regulated learning (SRL) and computer-based learning (CBL). They found evidence that some specific SRL processes were more often associated with academic success than others and that SRL skills could be supported. They also identified a number of issues that researchers should aim to address in future investigations, including more comprehensive measurement of facets of SRL and the quality of SRL processes, the potential disconnect between SRL processes and learning outcomes, and the distinction between self- and other-regulation.

A systematic review of the effects of scaffolding on SRL in science education in CBL was offered by Devolder et al. (2012). Scaffolding means providing temporary support for an inexperienced learner in order to help them to complete a task, acquire a skill, or part of a task or skill, then the support is gradually withdrawn as the student works towards independence. They analyzed 28 articles and noted that there was little clarity as to which types of scaffolds were most effective. Results showed that in the field of cognition, prompts appeared to be the most effective scaffolds. Individually ineffective scaffolds were domain-general, whereas effective scaffolds were both domain-general and domain-specific. Studies had paid little attention to scaffold designs, learner characteristics or task characteristics, or fading, despite the fact that these variables had been found to have a significant influence.

Zheng (2016) conducted a meta-analysis on the effects of SRL scaffolds on academic performance in computer-based learning environments. A total of 29 articles met the inclusion criteria, with a total sample size of 2648 students. Moderator analyses focused on three main areas of scaffold characteristics: the type of scaffold (including: the mechanism, functions, delivery forms, mode and number of scaffolds; how to promote self-regulated learning by scaffolds); demographics of the selected studies (including sample groups, sample size, learning domain, research settings and types of computer-based learning environments); and research methodological features (including research methods, types of research design, types of organization for treatment and duration of treatment). Findings revealed that SRL scaffolds in CBL environments generally produced a significantly positive effect on academic performance (ES = 0.44). Both domain-general and domain-specific scaffolds demonstrated substantial effects on academic performance.

A further systematic analysis of e-learning tools came from Garcia et al. (2018). A taxonomy of 14 categories of (SRL) strategies used by high school students had been proposed as long ago as 1986. However, at that time the categories did not consider SRL in digital environments. This review sought to understand if the original strategies were currently relevant in CBL and determine if new tools had emerged. A preponderance of research had been done on certain SRL skills, with limited focus on other categories.

Guo (2022) offered a meta-analysis specifically of using metacognitive prompts to enhance self-regulated learning in CBL. Prompts were typically delivered in the form of guiding questions, reflective questions and suggestions. Fixed prompts were held constant for all students, whereas adaptive prompts were customized to individual students' needs. Specific prompts were tailored to the task at hand and gave clear directions, but might come at the expense of making students feel constrained. Metacognitive prompts significantly enhanced SRL activities (ES = 0.50) and learning outcomes

(ES = 0.40) relative to control conditions. Moderator analyses revealed that the effects varied as a function of three features of the prompts (out of eight): feedback, specificity and adaptability. Developing task-specific, individual-adaptive prompts and feedback should be a design principle in CBL, such that the prompt effect could be retained, sustainably enhanced and transferred to novel situations.

A review paper by Mitsea et al. (2022) focused on students with disabilities and explored the extent to which fast learning was relevant to this population. The authors traced the essential indicators of speed learning with a special focus on those factors that were most relevant to learning disabilities. Then they presented evidence on training techniques and strategies that speeded up learning, exploring the role of information technology in speed learning. Speed learning training techniques improved all those factors that accelerated learning, such as spatial attention, visual span, processing speed, speed reaction, executive functions, metacognition and consciousness. Most important, fast learning strategies ameliorated control processes and spatial intelligence. Metacognition provided learners with meta-abilities needed to enter a state of peak performance. The study suggested including speed training strategies in schools to help students with or without disabilities.

Turning to individual studies, Azevedo et al. (2005) examined the effectiveness of three scaffolding conditions on adolescents' learning about the circulatory system with a hypermedia learning environment. One hundred and eleven adolescents were randomly assigned to one of three scaffolding conditions (adaptive scaffolding (AS), fixed scaffolding (FS), or no scaffolding (NS)) and were trained to use a hypermedia environment to learn about the circulatory system. Pre-test and post-test data measured qualitative changes in the students' mental models of the topic and quantitative changes in their declarative knowledge. Verbal protocols were collected during the 40-minute learning task to examine how each condition affected the way in which students regulated their learning. Findings revealed that learners in both the AS and NS conditions gained significantly more declarative knowledge than did those in the FS condition. Also, the AS condition was associated with significantly more shift in learners' mental models than the other conditions. Learners in the AS condition regulated their learning by planning and activating prior knowledge, monitoring their cognitive activities and their progress toward learning goals, using several effective strategies and engaging in adaptive help-seeking. Those in the NS condition used fewer effective strategies, while those in the FS condition regulated their learning by using several processes which actually seemed to impede their learning.

Lee et al. (2008) described the design and delivery of a 16-week course in major software packages at vocational schools in Taiwan. One class was a problem-based learning (PBL) class and the other was a non-PBL class. Each class had two groups divided according to whether the students were involved in SRL or not. A course website was devised and deployed to supplement learning activities in the traditional classroom. A series of quasi-experiments was conducted on web-enabled problem-based learning (PBL), self-regulated learning (SRL) and their combination. The impacts of these web-enabled pedagogies on students, instructors and course design were evaluated. Students' computing skills in terms of their average grades on three modules (Word, Excel, and PowerPoint) in the PBL class (67) were significantly higher than in the non-PBL class (57). The enhancement of computing skills in the SRL group (66) was significantly higher than that of the non-SRL group (58). The combination of PBL and SRL resulted in that group having the highest grades among the four groups.

A computer-based approach to enhance motivation and self-regulated learning was designed by Dresel and Haugwitz (2008). Participants were sixth-grade students ($n = 151$) who worked with a mathematics learning software program during regular classroom instruction. In the first condition, students received attributional software-generated feedback. In the second condition, students received the attributional feedback and additional self-regulation training. In a placebo/control condition, students received neither. Positive effects were seen on motivation and knowledge acquisition in both training conditions. An enhancement of metacognitive control strategies was evident only in the self-regulation condition. Moreover, the additional self-regulation training led to better knowledge acquisition than did the exclusive attributional feedback.

Wang (2011) developed a multiple-choice web-based assessment system, the Peer-Driven Assessment Module of the Web-based Assessment and Test Analysis system (PDA-WATA). The major purpose was to facilitate learner use of self-regulatory learning behaviors to improve e-learning effectiveness. PDA-WATA included five main strategies: Adding Answer Notes, Stating Confidence, Reading Peer Answer Notes, Recommending Peer Answer Notes and Querying Peers' Recommendation on Personal Answer Notes. Using these strategies, examinees could add answer notes to explain why they chose a certain option as the correct answer and state their confidence in their own answer and answer notes, for their peers' reference. Examinees could also recommend peer answer notes as valuable references and this could also be queried by all examinees. Participants were 123 seventh-grade junior high school students from four classes. These four classes were randomly divided into the PDA-WATA group (n = 63) and the Normal Web-Based Test (N-WBT) group (n = 60). After two weeks of e-learning instruction, results indicated PDA-WATA appeared significantly more effective than N-WBT in learner use of self-regulatory learning behaviors.

Specimen Program

The goal of the study by Zumbach et al. (2020) was to investigate the impact of metacognitive training, and metacognitive and cognitive prompting, in a game-based simulation related to demographic change. It focused on supporting learning with serious games by scaffolding students' self-regulated learning, fostering metacognition in constructivist learning environments. The impact of metacognitive training, and/or cognitive and metacognitive prompting, on learning outcomes and cognitive load was analyzed. A pre-test and post-test assessing knowledge acquisition, metacognitive behavior and cognitive load were applied. The learning environment was a game-based simulation of a small village that was confronted with different problems related to demographic change. Learners were tasked with developing sustainable solutions to keep the village prospering. With regard to knowledge acquisition, metacognitive and cognitive prompting proved effective, while the kind of direct metacognitive training used only had a minor effect. The results did not show a reduction of cognitive load through direct or indirect metacognitive and cognitive support. Taken together, outcomes suggest here that game-based learning with simulations can be supported by direct and indirect metacognitive and cognitive support.

Implementation

Learning with simulations or games requires interaction with the learning environment in order to generate, select, organize, and integrate information. Games can provide authentic practice, and thus provide the link between action and cognition. They also provide potential for team development, social learning and social cohesion, can enhance learner engagement and effort, provide a safe environment for learning and are adaptable to learner characteristics. The challenge of games should be adjusted to the increasing abilities and skills of learners. "Simply playing" educational games does not automatically lead to gains. Learners benefit more from game-based learning when additional instructional support is provided.

Learning with simulations or games is primarily self-regulated. Students' self-regulated learning may be fostered by the use of metacognitive strategies, either by direct instruction or more indirect prompting during learning, or both. However, it remains unclear under which conditions and in which domains metacognitive prompting might be applicable to and beneficial for learning. From a cognitive load perspective, the provision of an additional task during learning (e.g., metacognitive prompting) might reduce learners' capacity of working memory and, thus, inhibit rather than foster learning.

A total of 131 high school students aged between 14 and 17 voluntarily participated in this study (73 female, 58 male), randomly assigned to intervention or control groups. The overall duration of the intervention was 90 minutes. The game "Save the Village of Bauxdorf" was designed. Bauxdorf was a former mining village, a rural settlement affected by a dramatic decrease in inhabitants, whose mayor was trying to ensure the prosperity of the community. It was a learning simulation that offered a complex dynamic system with a high degree of authenticity. Finding solutions to the different problems presented required learners to define each problem and understand the complexity and different solution approaches that might be required as a result of conflicting interests of different protagonists. Learners were tasked with developing sustainable solutions to keep the village prospering. The game was set within a community council where different approaches to rescuing the village could be initiated and the consequences observed.

Participants were given detailed feedback on their decisions and opportunities to receive renewed system-generated feedback demonstrating the impact of these decisions and change or modify their problem-solving strategies. The learning environment did not need extra software skills beyond those expected after successfully finishing the sixth high school grade. Participants with metacognitive training received training on the nature and benefits of cognitive and metacognitive strategies, with examples, and subsequently had to write down examples of how they could apply these strategies. However, this training was very short. Prompts were given (see below).

List of metacognitive and cognitive prompts (For each type of prompt an example is given.)

Prompt 1:
  Activation of prior knowledge. Before you start learning, think about what you already know about demographic change.
  Cognitive. Have you heard about it before? If so, what topics and terms can you remember?

Prompts 2–4:
  Planning and evaluation of one's own progress. Think about what is required from you before you start the game. What is the stated problem?

Metacognitive and cognitive. How do you plan to solve the problem? What is your objective? Can you remember a similar learning situation? If so, think of how you have solved that problem in the past.

Please note the central terms of what you have seen. What is the central theme? What did you understand and what did you not understand? Have you ever heard about "push & pull factors"? Which other geography topics is this related to?

Prompt 5:
Evaluating the relevance of content for one's own objectives (cognitive). Which information is essential to the problem and your objectives, including for your further progress?

Prompt 6:
Detecting and resolving ambiguities (metacognitive). You have already made some important decisions. How did you decide on your problem-solving strategies?

Prompt 7:
Reflecting. Take a short break and think about your progress.

Metacognitive. Did you follow your plan? Have you tried to accomplish your objectives and tasks successfully?

Prompt 8:
Repetition and elaboration (cognitive). You have probably learned some new terms. Name the ones you remember and try to provide examples, e.g., migration within the country – a family moves from Salzburg to Linz.

Prompt 9:
You have completed the unit!
Evaluation of the learning process. Have you accomplished your objectives (both with regard to your task and your plan)?

Metacognitive and cognitive. Can you explain and use the central terms? What is still unclear?

In order to assess participants' knowledge before and after the intervention, a test comprising 12 multiple-choice questions and five open questions was developed. The cognitive and metacognitive learning strategies were measured with another questionnaire. The results revealed that the learning environment contributed to knowledge acquisition across all settings from pre- to post-test. However, the effects of the very brief training proved to be weak. There was a small but non-significant difference showing that participants who had received training reported a lower cognitive load. Metacognitive prompting showed a strong impact on knowledge acquisition.

References

Azevedo, R., Cromley, J. G., Winters, F. I., Moos, D. C., & Greene, J. A. (2005). Adaptive human scaffolding facilitates adolescents' self-regulated learning with hypermedia. *Instructional Science*, *33*, 381–412. doi: 10.1007/s11251-005-1273-8

Devolder, A., van Braak, J., & Tondeur, J. (2012). Supporting self-regulated learning in computer-based learning environments: Systematic review of effects of scaffolding in the domain of science education. *Journal of Computer Assisted Learning*, *28*(6), 557–573. doi: 10.1111/j.1365-2729.2011.00476.x

Dresel, M., & Haugwitz, M. (2008). A computer-based approach to fostering motivation and self-regulated learning. *The Journal of Experimental Education*, *77*(1), 3–20. doi: 10.3200/JEXE.77.1.3-20

Garcia, R., Falkner, K., & Vivian, R. (2018). Systematic literature review: Self-regulated learning strategies using e-learning tools for computer science. *Computers & Education*, *123*, 150–163. https://doi.org/10.1016/j.compedu.2018.05.006

Guo, L. (2022). Using metacognitive prompts to enhance self-regulated learning and learning outcomes: A meta-analysis of experimental studies in computer-based learning environments. *Journal of Computer Assisted Learning*, *38*, 811–832. doi: 10.1111/jcal.12650

Lee, T. H., Shen, P. D., & Tsai, C. W. (2008). Applying web-enabled problem-based learning and self-regulated learning to add value to computing education in Taiwan's vocational schools. *Educational Technology & Society*, *11*(3), 13–25. https://www.jstor.org/stable/10.2307/jeductechsoci.11.3.13

Mitsea, E., Drigas, A., & Skianis, C. (2022). ICTs and speed learning in special education: High-consciousness training strategies for high-capacity learners through metacognition lens. *Technium Social Sciences Journal*, *27*, 230–252. doi: 10.47577/tssj.v27i1.5599

Wang, T. H. (2011). Developing web-based assessment strategies for facilitating junior high school students to perform self-regulated learning in an e-learning environment. *Computers & Education*, *57*, 1801–1812. doi: 10.1016/j.compedu.2011.01.003

Winters, F. I., Greene, J. A., & Costich, C. M. (2008). Self-regulation of learning within computer-based learning environments: A critical analysis. *Educational Psychology Review*, *20*, 429–444. https://doi.org/10.1007/s10648-008-9080-9

Zheng, L. Q. (2016). The effectiveness of self-regulated learning scaffolds on academic performance in computer-based learning environments: A meta-analysis. *Asia Pacific Educational Review*, *17*, 187–202. doi: 10.1007/s12564-016-9426-9

Zumbach, J., Rammerstorfer, L., & Deibl, I. (2020). Cognitive and metacognitive support in learning with a serious game about demographic change. *Computers in Human Behavior*, *103*, 120–129. https://doi.org/10.1016/j.chb.2019.09.026

20
Metacognition and Artificial Intelligence

The origins of artificial intelligence (AI) lie back in the 1950s, when Alan Turing wrote: "I propose to consider the question whether or not it is possible for machinery to show intelligent behavior." In 1956 John McCarthy convened a conference to discuss the concept and the term AI was coined.

Now we are very familiar with AI, although we might not always recognize it. Some well-known applications are: advanced web search engines (e.g., Google Search), targeting online advertisements (to personally focus advertisements based on your past usage), recommendation systems (suggesting things in which you might be interested, used by YouTube, Amazon and Netflix), understanding human speech (e.g., Siri, Alexa and Google Assistant), automatic language translation (such as Microsoft Translator and Google Translate), self-driving cars (e.g., Waymo and Tesla), generative or creative tools for text or graphics (such as ChatGPT, Microsoft Bing, Google Bard, Perplexity, Hugging Chat and AI art), facial recognition (such as Apple's Face ID or Microsoft's DeepFace), image labeling (used by Facebook, Apple's iPhoto and TikTok), and competing at the highest level in strategic games (such as chess and Go). The increasing realism and ease of use of AI-based text-to-image generators such as Midjourney, DALL-E and Stable Diffusion has sparked a trend of viral AI-generated photos. However, fiction has always been ahead of reality, as with HAL 9000, the murderous "Heuristically-programmed ALgorithmic" computer in charge of the spaceship in Stanley Kubrick's 1968 film *2001: A Space Odyssey*.

AI may help teachers make better decisions because computers notice patterns that teachers can miss. For example, when a teacher and student agree that the student needs reminders, an AI system may provide reminders in whatever form a student likes without adding to the teacher's workload. Personalization tools may automatically adjust the sequence, pace, hints or trajectory through learning experiences. An AI-enabled assistant may appear as an additional "partner" to a small group of students who are working together on a collaborative assignment. However, exercising judgment and control in the use of AI is an essential part of providing the best opportunity to learn for all students. AI does not have the broad qualities of contextual judgment that people do, so people must remain responsible for education.

Universities have already developed policies for managing AI use among their students. Typically, they permit AI use in developing or researching topics, but require that the final product is all the student's own work. Of course, plagiarism from published sources has for many years been assessed by software such as TurnItIn, Grammarly, ProWritingAid, WriterZen, Quetext and PlagiarismCheck, but whether such software can handle AI-generated written products is another question, unless all students using AI on a particular topic get the same AI product. These developments will likely cascade down into schools.

AI can have a high degree of complexity, which may challenge students, especially when they are new to it or are of lower ability. Consequently, many authors have argued that enhanced metacognition and self-regulated learning (SRL) are crucial in AI, particularly goal-setting, prompting, self-assessment, feedback and personalization. AI can also provide learning analytics to help learners reflect on their SRL strategies. Safety with AI has also become an important concern and metacognition is likely to help with this. However, in the flurry of attention devoted to AI, we should not forget that human intelligence is very important and enhancing human critical and creative thinking skills is just as if not more crucial.

Definition

Artificial intelligence (AI) is the ability of a computer (or a robot controlled by a computer) to do tasks that are usually done by humans because they (used to) require human intelligence (such as reasoning and learning), or that involve data whose scale exceeds what humans are able to analyze. AI is the simulation of human intelligence processes by machines, especially computers. Specific applications of AI include expert systems, visual perception, natural language processing, speech recognition, decision making and translation between languages.

While AI clearly has advantages, there are also disadvantages, one of which is the lack of transparency. Most AI applications cannot explain how they have reached a decision. Their complexity makes it difficult for even an expert to explain how they produced their outputs. Consequently, their reliability always seems to be in question. AI also provides a number of tools that are particularly useful for authoritarian governments: Smart spyware, face recognition and voice recognition allow widespread surveillance; such surveillance allows classification of potential enemies of the state and can prevent them from hiding; recommendation systems can precisely target propaganda and misinformation for maximum effect; deepfakes aid in producing misinformation; and so on.

Background

Tools

First, we will take a look at some of the AI tools that are available in education, to give readers a feel of what we are talking about. An early initiative was that of Azevedo et al. (2009), who outlined the theoretical and conceptual assumptions of self-regulated learning (SRL) underlying MetaTutor, a hypermedia environment designed to train and foster students' SRL processes in biology. The deployment of key cognitive and metacognitive regulatory processes was key to enhancing learning in open-ended learning environments such as hypermedia.

Lin (2022) presented IdiomsTube, a computer-assisted language learning tool for facilitating the learning of English idiomatic expressions from YouTube videos. The web-based tool was designed to automatically: (1) assess the speech rate and lexical difficulty level of any learner-chosen English-captioned YouTube video; (2) generate a range of vocabulary-building and revision tasks (e.g., fill-in-the-blanks, the classic spelling game hangman, pronunciation, flashcards); and (3) recommend further YouTube videos based on learners' individual learning progress, class teachers' instructions and current trends.

The RiPPLE platform was described by Darvishi et al. (2022). It relied on learner-sourcing, which involved students in the creation and evaluation of a variety of learning resources. Users could create multiple-choice questions, multiple-answer questions, working examples and open-ended notes, which had to go through a peer assessment procedure. Peer assessors were requested to evaluate the quality of student-generated content using a multiple-criteria rubric that instructors could customize for each resource type. Before submitting their assessment, assessors were required to support their judgment and offer comments to the author.

Swiecki et al. (2022) reviewed a number of AI assessment tools which could enhance metacognition. Software to support peer assessment included platforms such as Mechanical TA, Dear Beta and Dear Gamma, Aropa and Crowd-Grader. Additionally, systems for automated essay scoring had been used, such as MI Write, which offered a web-based interactive system for students to practice and improve their writing skills. For every essay, MI Write provided the student with an overall score for the essay and six sub-scores (development of ideas, organization, style, word choice, sentence fluency, and conventions). Several studies had demonstrated that automated essay scoring could help students improve their writing motivation, self-efficacy and skills.

Electronic assessment platforms provided the possibility for exams to be administered on- or offline. AI research had already investigated: measuring and classifying test-taking effort; answering and revising behavior during exams; metacognitive regulation of strategies and cognitive processing; detecting rapid-guessing and pre-knowledge behaviors; modeling examinees' accuracy, speed and revisits; modeling students in real-time while taking a self-assessment; and understanding students' performance in various contexts such as complex problem solving.

Beyond this, "stealth assessment" techniques collected data automatically from the process of learners' interaction with a task, to be able to investigate more than whether students' answers were correct. Also of interest was authentic assessment, measuring learning using tasks that simulated those undertaken by actual members of some community of practice. For example, in simulations called virtual internships, learners intern at a fictional company where they work in teams to design a product. The goal is to give learners scaffolded experience of doing the kinds of things that professionals actually do.

Reviews

There are many reviews of AI in education, but fewer which relate AI to metacognition. An early review by Azevedo and Witherspoon (2009) argued that metacognition was especially necessary in a hypermedia environment. Even earlier reviews had suggested that most hypermedia learning studies focused too much on final products and not enough on how learners achieved them. Several key self-regulatory processes had been identified. First, there were planning processes such as activating prior knowledge, setting and coordinating sub-goals that pertained to accessing new information, and defining which problem solution steps to perform for accomplishing a complex task. There were also several monitoring processes deployed during task enactment, including monitoring one's understanding of the topic, managing the learning environment and other instructional resources necessary to accomplish the learning goals and engaging in periodic self-assessment. During task performance a learner must also use several effective learning strategies, such as coordinating several informational sources (e.g., text, diagram, animations), generating hypotheses, extracting relevant information from resources, re-reading, making inferences, summarizing and re-representing the topic based on emerging understanding by taking notes and drawing. Lastly, the learner must continuously adjust during learning by handling task difficulties and demands such as monitoring progress towards goals and modifying the amount of time and effort necessary to complete the learning task.

These self-regulatory monitoring processes were identified as: Feeling of Knowing (FOK), Judgment of Learning (JOL), Monitoring Use of Strategies (MUS), Self-Test (ST), Monitoring Progress Toward Goals (MPTG), Time Monitoring (TM), Content Evaluation (CE) and Evaluation of Adequacy of Content (EAC). The three most frequently used were FOK, JOL and CE.

In 2020 Atun also focused on Intelligent Tutoring Systems (ITS), noting they differed from traditional computer-assisted learning in that the system could change itself according to data it got from students and teachers. His systematic review of 11 articles on the development of reading comprehension skill in primary and secondary education with ITSs found in all cases that they were more effective than traditional teaching methods. There was only one study in secondary education. Students with a low reading level tended to do better with ITSs. The ITS known as Text Structure Strategy was the most common one in studies, while others were TuinLEC, iSTART, iSTART-ME and LODE (a logic-based tool for deaf children).

Drigas et al. (2022) reviewed 25 articles with a total of 1073 participants about virtual reality (VR) and metacognition training for students with learning disabilities. (Virtual reality is the computer-generated simulation of a three-dimensional image or environment that can be interacted with in a seemingly real or physical way by a person using special electronic equipment, such as a helmet with a screen inside or gloves fitted with sensors.) They emphasized the advantages of VR in clinical hypnosis, neurolinguistic programming, subliminal training, fast learning and mindfulness. There was evidence of beneficial effects on learning disabilities, cognitive impairments, autism,

ADHD (Attention Deficit Hyperactivity Disorder), depression, generalized anxiety disorder, phobias and behavioral and emotional disorders. Metacognitive abilities could be directly trained through VR.

Individual Studies

Roll et al. (2011) investigated whether immediate metacognitive feedback on students' help-seeking errors could assist students in acquiring better help-seeking skills. The Help Tutor, an intelligent tutor agent for help seeking, was integrated into a tutoring system for geometry, the Geometry Cognitive Tutor. One study with 58 students found the Help Tutor improved students' help-seeking behavior while using the Geometry Cognitive Tutor. A second study with 67 students evaluated more elaborated support that included help-seeking instruction and support for self-assessment, which again found positive results. The improved help-seeking skills also transferred to the month following the intervention.

iSTART, a reading comprehension AI strategy, was the focus of work by McCarthy et al. (2018). In iSTART students practiced writing quality self-explanations. Self-assessment prompted students to estimate their self-explanation score and students were notified when their average self-explanation score was below a required threshold. Students who practiced with iSTART had higher post-test self-explanation scores and inference comprehension scores than control students.

Wang et al. (2022) deployed a mathematics metacognitive intelligence assessment and strategy implementation AI system for 2100 middle school students. This could intelligently assess students' mathematical metacognition level and propose targeted improvement strategies. The results showed that experimental participants had advantages in mathematical metacognitive knowledge and metacognitive management.

The moderating effects of need satisfaction and gender in predicting SRL with a chatbot among grade 9 students were examined by Xia et al. (2022). (A chatbot is a computer program that simulates and processes written or spoken human conversation, allowing humans to interact with digital devices as if they were communicating with a real person.) The girls perceived stronger needs for support regarding autonomy, competence and relatedness than the boys. Particularly among girls, the effects of autonomy and competence more strongly predicted SRL when AI knowledge was low.

Li et al. (2023) used a chatbot in flipped mathematics classrooms (a flipped classroom is a type of blended learning, which has students interact with readings or online learning at home and then work on live problem-solving during class time) to provide personalized learning to improve self-regulation issues that students faced when learning at home. The accuracy of ChatGPT was tested, using it to answer questions from past examinations, and accuracy was found as high as 90% (equivalent to an A+ grade). Moreover, ChatGPT's accuracy in each of the six major areas of mathematics education exceeded 80% (grade A).

Specimen Program

Matsuda et al. (2020) compared the effect of AI-delivered metacognitive scaffolding for learning against the effect of learning by tutoring a synthetic peer. Three versions of an online learning environment for learning algebra linear equations were created: (1) APLUS (Artificial Peer Learning Environment Using SimStudent) which allowed students to interactively teach a synthetic peer with the goal to have that synthetic peer pass a quiz while the system provided tutors with metacognitive scaffolding on how to teach; (2) APLUSTUTOR which provided cognitive tutoring (i.e., immediate feedback and just-in-time hint) and metacognitive scaffolding on how to learn; and (3) COGTUTOR+ which provided traditional cognitive tutoring on mastery learning. Two school studies were conducted with a total of 444 sixth- to eighth-grade students. The results showed that: (i) students' proficiency in solving equations increased after using the interventions for four days, but there was no difference in effectiveness across the three interventions, and (ii) learning by teaching with metacognitive scaffolding facilitated learning equally across various levels of students' prior competency. AI tutoring was as effective in all conditions. Of course, human peer tutoring results in gains for the tutor as well as the tutee and AI does not meet this double gain criterion.

Implementation

Two classroom studies were conducted where three different learning strategies were compared: Learning by Teaching (APLUS), Goal-Oriented Practice (APLUSTUTOR) and Cognitive Tutoring (COGTUTOR+). In addition to the learning outcome data (test scores), detailed learning process data (that showed interactions between students and an online learning system) were collected.

APLUS (Artificial Peer Learning Environment Using SimStudent) was an online learning environment where students learned to solve equations by teaching a synthetic peer. The synthetic peer was visualized as an avatar in the lower left corner. Prior to using APLUS, students could customize the avatar by changing its hair style, skin color and shirt color. The image of the avatar's face was gender-neutral. Students could also name it.

SimStudent was an agent that interactively learned skills to solve problems through guided problem solving, i.e., a student using APLUS acted as a tutor for SimStudent. SimStudent applied inductive logic programming to induce skills in the form of production rules by generalizing given examples. The basic tutoring interactions between a student and SimStudent included the following: (1) A student posed a problem (of their choice from a problem bank or one they made up) for SimStudent to solve. (2) SimStudent attempted to solve the problem. Each step performed by SimStudent was shown on the Tutoring Interface. SimStudent then asked the student for feedback on its correctness. SimStudent was pre-trained on a few one-step equations before students started tutoring so that it had reached a certain level of background knowledge. Thus, SimStudent might initially perform steps both correctly and incorrectly. (3) The student provided yes/no feedback on the correctness of the step performed by SimStudent. When the student said "no" to

SimStudent's step, SimStudent then made another attempt by applying an alternative skill, if any. (4) When SimStudent had no skills to apply, SimStudent asked the student for help. The student had to demonstrate the step by entering an expression in the Tutoring Interface. (5) The student might quiz SimStudent at any time during tutoring by clicking on the [Quiz] button. SimStudent applied productions learned thus far to solve quiz problems.

The goal for students using APLUS was to have their SimStudent pass the quiz. The quiz had four sections ordered by difficulty – One Step Equation (1 problem), Two Step Equation (2 problems), Equations with Variables on Both Sides (4 problems), and Final Challenge (8 problems which were all equations with variables on both sides). When the [Quiz] button was clicked, SimStudent solved a single problem at a time. When the problem was solved, the individual steps made by SimStudent were displayed along with the correctness of each step.

The Cognitive Tutor graded the quiz results (it did not interact with the student – it was used only for quiz and logging purposes). For each section of the quiz, SimStudent had to complete the section by solving all problems correctly to proceed to the next section. To "pass" the quiz, SimStudent had to complete all quiz sections. Students therefore had to teach SimStudent sufficient skills to solve equations with variables on both sides to achieve the goal. When a problem was completed, SimStudent occasionally checked the solution by plugging the solution into the original equation and seeing if the equation balanced. The solution checking happened randomly with 30% chance. This function was introduced because it was observed that students taught SimStudent incorrectly (hence leading to an incorrect solution) without knowing they had made a mistake. By checking the solution, SimStudent could at least bring an error to the student's attention. The solution checking was implemented as a think-aloud monologue by SimStudent.

There were learning resources available for students to review: (1) Unit Overview, which provided a brief overview of how to solve algebra equations, (2) Examples which provided worked-out examples for the target equations, (3) Intro Video, which was a brief video explaining how to use APLUS, and (4) Problem Bank, which provided a list of suggested equations to be used for teaching.

APLUS included a teacher agent (also known as a meta-tutor) called Mr. Williams, visualized with an avatar on the lower right corner of the APLUS interface. Unlike the SimStudent avatar, the Mr. Williams avatar could not be changed and it always appeared. Mr. Williams provided students with help on how to appropriately tutor SimStudent (called metacognitive tutoring help) for the following five metacognitive skills of tutoring identified as most troublesome for students: (1) Selecting an appropriate next problem to teach to SimStudent – Mr. Williams suggested the student teach a problem from the quiz that SimStudent failed to solve. An example of a help message from Mr. Williams for the problem selection read: "I see that Tom failed all quiz items. Tom can do better with some practice on two-step equations"; (2) Administering the quiz at an appropriate time – after teaching SimStudent, Mr. Williams suggested the student administer the quiz to SimStudent. An example of a help message from Mr. Williams for the quiz read: "I see Tom passed this quiz section – it might be helpful to understand what else your student knows. So, it would be a good idea to quiz Tom again now." (3) Reviewing resources, e.g., Unit Overview and Examples, at an appropriate time – when SimStudent did not make any progress on the quiz, Mr. Williams suggested the student review the resources. An example of a help message from Mr. Williams for reviewing resources read: "I think it's a good idea to go through the Examples – see the tab above. Make sure you understand all the examples." (4) Providing feedback – when SimStudent was asking the student for feedback on the step it performed, Mr. Williams suggested the student provide yes/no feedback. An example of a help message from Mr. Williams for providing feedback read: "Tom is asking you to justify your answer. You should answer Tom's question." (5) Demonstrating a step on which SimStudent got stuck – when SimStudent was asking the student for help on how to perform the next step, Mr. Williams suggested the student enter a corresponding step in the Tutoring Interface. An example of a help message from Mr. Williams for demonstration read: "Tom is asking for help. You should tell Tom the next step."

The metacognitive tutoring help was delivered either by request or proactively. Students could click on Mr. Williams anytime to ask their questions about how to teach. When Mr. Williams was clicked, a pop-up menu was then shown with available questions for the student to ask. Mr. Williams also occasionally provided hints proactively (without the student's request). Both for requested and proactive hints, a hint message from Mr. Williams was displayed in a separate dialog box so that students could perceive it as a private message.

COGTUTOR+ was a cognitive tutor which had the same graphical user interface as APLUS. It provided the student with mastery learning. COGTUTOR+ was designed so that it provided adaptive instruction, i.e., immediate feedback, just-in-time hint and adaptive problem selection. The first two types of adaptive instruction (immediate feedback and just-in-time hint) compared students' solutions with model solutions. There were nine skills that were involved, all of which were the same skills that SimStudent learned on APLUS.

Each step a student entered in the Tutoring Interface of COGTUTOR+ was colored either red, which indicated that the step was incorrect, or green, which indicated that the step was correct. While using COGTUTOR+, the student could ask for a just-in-time hint for the next correct step (e.g., "What should I do next?") by clicking on Mr. Williams. The third type of adaptive instruction (adaptive problem selection) computed the mastery level of individual skills as the probability of applying them correctly.

The goal for a student using COGTUTOR+ was to achieve a mastery proficiency level for all nine skills across all types of equations that were the same as in APLUS – one-step equation, two-step equation and equations with variables on both sides. Students' progress on the proficiency level was displayed as a bar graph on the right-hand side of the COGTUTOR+ interface. It showed an average of the proficiency of the skill learning for each quiz level. COGTUTOR+ was designed to control for the learning resources for students to review with APLUS – i.e., the same Intro Video, Unit Overview and worked-out Examples as for APLUS were available. However, there was no metacognitive help provided by COGTUTOR+ to suggest when students should review these resources.

APLUSTUTOR was a cognitive tutor that provided the same adaptive instruction as COGTUTOR+, i.e., immediate feedback and just-in-time hint. The same nine skills used for APLUS and COGTUTOR+ were used for APLUSTUTOR. Unlike COGTUTOR+, adaptive problem selection was not provided by APLUSTUTOR. Instead, students chose problems from the Problem Bank or made them up and entered them into the Tutoring Interface by themselves. APLUSTUTOR did not compute students' mastery level – the goal for students was to solve all quiz problems correctly by themselves. The quiz sections in APLUSTUTOR were organized in the same way as in APLUS. The student could click on the [Quiz] tab to take a quiz at any time. The student was asked to submit a solution for one quiz problem at a time (just like SimStudent solved a single quiz problem at a time) and the system provided feedback on the correctness of the solution. The student could modify an incorrect solution and resubmit as many times as they wanted. The interface of APLUSTUTOR was almost identical to APLUS except there was no synthetic peer present. A student entered a problem in the interface and then adaptive scaffolding was provided (i.e., immediate feedback and just-in-time hint), while the student was solving the problem. Students could click on Mr. Williams anytime to ask for a hint. In addition to the just-in-time hint, Mr. Williams also provided the following three types of metacognitive hints that were equivalent to the metacognitive tutoring help provided by APLUS: (1) Selecting an appropriate next problem to practice, (2) Taking the quiz at an appropriate time, (3) Reviewing resources. Like APLUS, these types of metacognitive hints were delivered either upon students' request or proactively by Mr. Williams.

For one study, two public schools participated with a total of 184 seventh- and eighth-grade students in 12 algebra classrooms. For the other, one public school participated with a total of 260 sixth- and seventh-grade students in 12 algebra classrooms. Three study conditions were implemented: (1) APLUS,

(2) COGTUTOR+ and (3) APLUSTUTOR. Both studies were randomized controlled trials based on within-class randomization – i.e., in each classroom, individual students were randomly assigned to one condition. Students' learning activity was measured using learning process data automatically collected by the system. Interactions included problems used for tutoring or practice, solutions entered by the student and the synthetic peer, quiz progress, hints requested, and so on. The correctness of each step made by students and the synthetic peer was judged and logged.

The results from both studies showed that by adding metacognitive scaffolding there was no longer any tendency for students with low prior competency to benefit more from learning by being tutored. Regardless of this, there was generally no difference between the three conditions for the level of proficiency achieved after using the interventions for four days. Of course, use for a longer time period might have resulted in differences.

References

Atun, H. (2020). Intelligent Tutoring Systems (ITS) to improve reading comprehension: A systematic review. *Journal of Teacher Education and Lifelong Learning*, *2*(2), 77–89. https://dergipark.org.tr/en/pub/tell/issue/58491/757329

Azevedo, R., & Witherspoon, A. M. (2009). Self-regulated learning with hypermedia. In D. J. Hacker, J. Dunlosky & A. C. Graesser (Eds.), *Handbook of Metacognition in Education* (pp. 319–339). New York and London: Routledge.

Azevedo, R., Witherspoon, A., Chauncey, A., Burkett, C., & Fike, A. (2009). MetaTutor: A metacognitive tool for enhancing self-regulated learning. *Cognitive and Metacognitive Educational Systems: Papers from the AAAI Fall Symposium*. https://cdn.aaai.org/ocs/995/995-4214-1-PB.pdf

Darvishi, A., Khosravi, H., Sadiq, S., & Gašević, D. (2022). Incorporating AI and learning analytics to build trustworthy peer assessment systems. *British Journal of Educational Technology*, *53*, 844–875. doi: 10.1111/bjet.13233

Drigas, A., Mitsea, E., & Skianis, C. (2022). Virtual reality and metacognition training techniques for learning disabilities. *Sustainability*, *14*, 10170. https://doi.org/10.3390/su141610170

Li, P. H., Lee, H. Y., Cheng, Y. P., Starčič, A. I., & Huang, Y. M. (2023). Solving the self-regulated learning problem: Exploring the performance of ChatGPT in mathematics. In Y. M. Huang & T. Rocha (Eds.), *Innovative Technologies and Learning. ICITL 2023*. Lecture Notes in Computer Science, vol. 14099. Champaign, IL: Springer. https://doi.org/10.1007/978-3-031-40113-8_8

Lin, P. (2022). Developing an intelligent tool for computer-assisted formulaic language learning from YouTube videos. *ReCALL*, *34*(2), 185–200. doi: 10.1017/S0958344021000252

McCarthy, K. S., Likens, A. D., Johnson, A. M., Guerrero, T. A., & McNamara, D. S. (2018). Metacognitive overload! Positive and negative effects of metacognitive prompts in an Intelligent Tutoring System. *International Journal of Artificial Intelligence in Education*, *28*, 420–438. https://doi.org/10.1007/s40593-018-0164-5

Matsuda, N., Weng, W. T., & Wall, N. (2020). The effect of metacognitive scaffolding for learning by teaching a teachable agent. *International Journal of Artificial Intelligence in Education*, *30*, 1–37. https://doi.org/10.1007/s40593-019-00190-2

Roll, I., Aleven, V., McLaren, B. M., & Koedinger, K. R. (2011). Improving students' help-seeking skills using metacognitive feedback in an intelligent tutoring system. *Learning and Instruction*, *21(2)*, 267–280. https://doi.org/10.1016/j.learninstruc.2010.07.004

Swiecki, Z., Khosravi, H., Chen, G. L., Martinez-Maldonado, R., Lodge, J. M., Milligan, S., Selwyn, N., & Găsevíc, D. (2022). Assessment in the age of artificial intelligence. *Computers and Education: Artificial Intelligence*, *3*, 100075. https://doi.org/10.1016/j.caeai.2022.100075

Wang, G., Kang, Y., Jiao, Z., Chen, X., Zhen, Y., Zhang, D., & Su, M. (2022). Development and application of intelligent assessment system for metacognition in learning mathematics among junior high school students. *Sustainability*, *14*, 6278. https://doi.org/10.3390/su14106278

Xia, Q., Chiu T. K. F., & Chai, C. S. (2023). The moderating effects of gender and need satisfaction on self-regulated learning through Artificial Intelligence (AI). *Education and Information Technologies*, *28*, 8691–8713. https://doi.org/10.1007/s10639-022-11547-x

Section F
Discussion and Conclusion

21

Discussion and Conclusion

This final chapter offers a discussion of the common threads that these metacognitive techniques share. This may be suitable for busy school managers or politicians to read first.

Each metacognitive technique has been mentioned in its own section, but it may also be mentioned in other sections. In addition, some metacognitive techniques and other important issues which do not have their own section may be mentioned. Consequently, an inspection of each of the chapters from 2 through 20 for mentions of techniques has been made, leading to a count of the most popular techniques. The numbers of mentions of each is given in brackets in the following text. Only the evidence-based sections of each chapter were searched (i.e., the Background and Specimen Program sections). A discussion of the utility of each technique and relations between techniques ensues. Remember all of these techniques have demonstrated evidence of effectiveness.

Metacognitive Techniques Which Had Their Own Chapter

An early preoccupation with metacognitive knowledge has now been displaced by a much stronger focus on metacognitive skills (4), and in particular on Self-Regulated Learning (SRL) (31), which had the highest number of mentions and was related to Decision

Making (7). Thus, the emphasis has shifted from knowing about metacognition to actually doing metacognition. SRL implies wide-ranging application of metacognitive skills, but few studies have actually measured operation in more than one subject domain and at most in three. Self-Regulation and Decision-Making may be negatively associated with procrastination, which may be intentional and strategic or implicit and potentially damaging.

Among the specific techniques, Self-Assessment (18), Questioning (16), Visualization (16) (which was also associated with Diagrams (7)), interaction with Memory (15) and Memory and Disability (14) all came out strongly. Self-Assessment implies not only assessing the product of the task, but more importantly the efficiency of the process of achieving success in the task, and may use rubrics to heighten awareness of the criteria against which both products and process are to be assessed. Questioning is of course at least as old as Socrates, but is still an important component in metacognition, both in answering metacognitive questions from the teacher or peers and in being able to develop metacognitive questions for others to answer. Visualization and Diagrams have long been associated with metacognition and can be static or dynamic, working to decrease cognitive load, but of course preference for this type of method may be specific to some kinds of learners, while others prefer continuous text. Memory and metacognition interact, as memory is necessary to apply many metacognitive skills and impaired memory can affect metacognitive capability. This is particularly important with students with Learning Disability and/or Attention Deficit Hyperactivity Disorder. Memory training or metacognitive training might improve this, or preferably both. Computerized and Online Learning (14) methods often reflected methods where delivery was digitalized merely for convenience or application at scale, whereas Artificial Intelligence methods (14) were more likely to offer fundamentally novel approaches.

Next came Dialog (10), Think-Aloud (9) and Predictions (10). After this came Mnemonics (8), Modeling (7), Peer Assessment (6) and Summarizing (6). Of course, some of these counts are affected by current popularity rather than effectiveness or growth potential. Dialog may be with the teacher or more likely with peers (where lower effectiveness may be balanced by greater opportunities for interaction). Think-Aloud has been a popular method for investigating metacognitive processes, but it is also a means of heightening metacognitive processes. Predictions and Mnemonics might seem somewhat old-fashioned, but have sustained their popularity and seem effective. Modeling has two aspects, both teacher modeling or demonstrating metacognitive thinking and also abstract demonstration (often visual) of how a system operates. Summarizing has perhaps unfairly gone out of fashion as a topic for researchers, while Peer Assessment is currently less used than Self-Assessment, but may well expand in the future and/or be more used together with Self-Assessment, as Peer Assessment offers the perspective of others which may be a corrective to a biased self-assessment.

Some of these elements featured in the previous associated book about enhancing cognition. Particularly, Peer Interaction (10) and Discourse, Dialog and Argumentation (9) figure in both books (numbers in brackets indicate number of mentions in the first book). Modeling (7) and Scaffolding (7) also feature in both books, as do Questioning (5), Prediction (5) and Judgment or Decision Making (5). Also featuring in both books were Self-Esteem and Self-Efficacy (5), Strategies and Heuristics (4), Diagrams, Graphic Organizers and Concept Maps (4), Summarizing (3) and the importance of Training (2).

Other Metacognitive Techniques and Overall Model

In the early stages of exploration of metacognitive methods, a simple model of metacognitive functioning was proposed, involving merely Planning, Monitoring and Evaluation (see Figure 21.1). Indeed, even quite recently this was regarded as a key model in metacognition (e.g., Veenman, 2015). Consequently, Planning (7), Monitoring (10) and Evaluation (2) appeared as key concepts in the metacognition search, even though they were not assigned their own chapter. The problem was that they were very vague

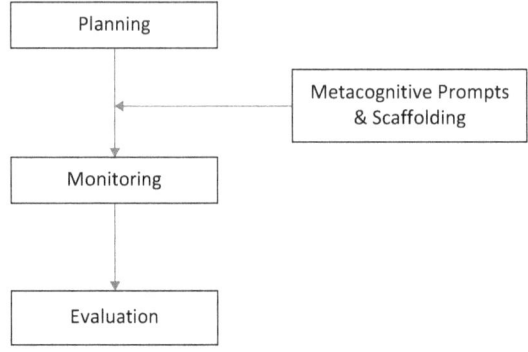

FIGURE 21.1 A simple model of metacognition

and general, and were usually investigated all together rather than separately. Importantly for teachers, they did nothing to suggest how metacognition should be implemented, i.e., what teachers should do with classes in order to get from Planning to Monitoring.

With Metacognitive Prompts (10) and Scaffolding (7), teachers began to obtain some idea of how to move from Planning to Monitoring. These methods again were very vague and general and often embedded within a particular subject. Thus, although these also do not have their own chapter, they are very fully discussed in Chapter 2 on Science.

However, this book goes considerably beyond this simple model in elaborating ways in which teachers can move from Planning to Monitoring, filling the implementation gap. This gives us an elaborated model of metacognition, as described in Figure 21.2. The final goal of all metacognitive strategies is to develop Self-Regulation and Decision Making (Chapter 16), which can be applied to all subjects in school and to issues arising out of school and indeed in later life. To achieve this goal, teachers can choose from the array of evidence-based methods in the left-hand column of the figure, each of which has its own chapter.

These two figures exemplify both Modeling (Chapter 8) and Visualization (Chapter 10), of course.

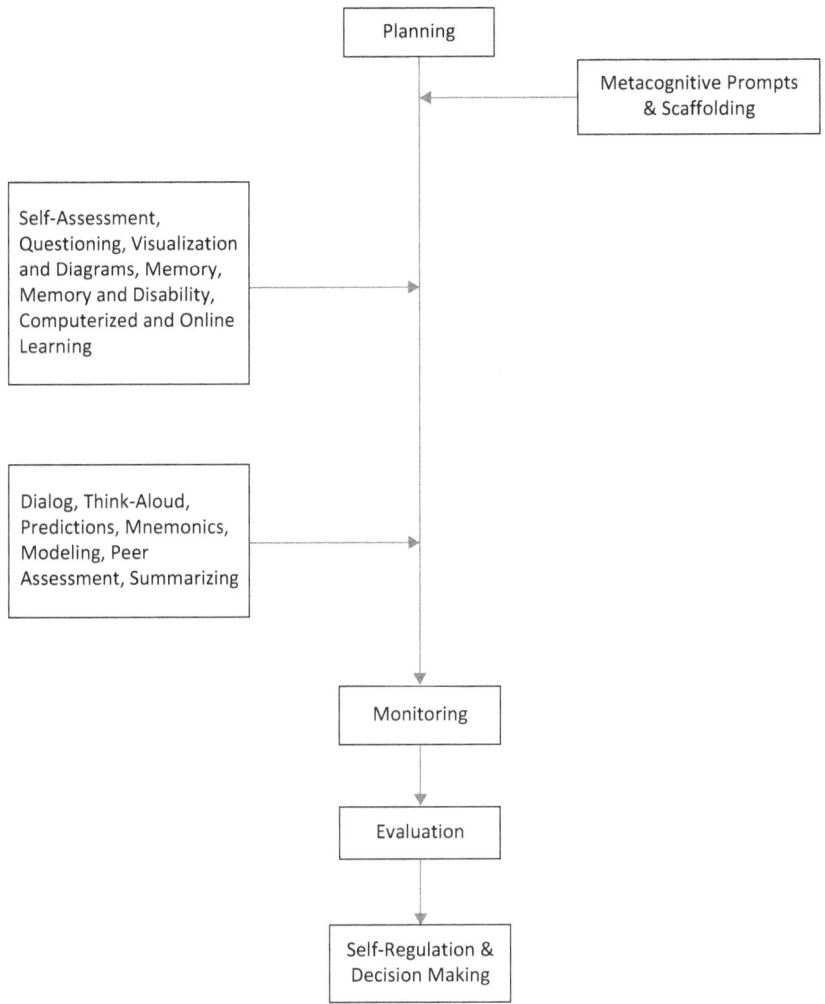

FIGURE 21.2 A more complex model of metacognition

Other Issues

The inspection of the chapters flagged a number of other issues which may be of interest to readers. The most mentioned of these was the importance of training (19). Some authors approached this via direct instruction (3), others via a less teacher-centered and more student-centered approach, some by both methods. In all cases, it was important that students were not seen as blank slates (3) and previous faulty learning might have to be undone. Coupled with this was the role of practice (3) – as with any skill, instruction was just the start and students would improve with practice.

One thing that also would likely improve with practice and time was student self-efficacy (12) or self-confidence, which was emphasized by many authors. Initially even the teacher's self-confidence would not be high, but this would develop with increasing success. Coupled with this was the role of motivation (9), which initially might be poor or confused, until the experience of success enhanced it.

Other operational factors might be important. Do studies show long-term effects (6)? A minority of studies investigated this issue, but most found that there were long-term effects. Does gender (6) make a difference? Many studies investigating this found no difference between genders, while others found girls superior and/or boys inferior. Does the age of the students (4) make a difference? It might be somewhat easier to enhance metacognition in older students who are more conceptually mature, but they also have more previous faulty learning. There are some studies showing the former effect, but also many successful studies with very young children. Does the ability of the students (3) make a difference (since it might be difficult to explain metacognitive concepts to low-ability students)? Results here are various – some found high-ability students did better while others found low-ability students did better. Does the time length of the intervention (3) make a difference? Well, not really, since some studies actually found shorter interventions more effective. Finally, the most important question – is there not only maintenance of intervention effects in the subject of choice, but is there generalization of effects (5) to other subjects and issues? Studies that investigated this confirmed that generalization was possible.

Conclusion

The journey we want our students to take starts with acquiring metacognitive knowledge, proceeds to developing metacognitive skills and stimulates the students to be self-regulated learners. We want them to do this in one subject domain, generalize it to other subject domains and then to all kinds of problems and issues beyond and after school. However, we should not regard them as blank slates – they may already have some metacognitive skills, probably at the subconscious or implicit level, and we need to bring these out.

The teacher's role is crucial, but it is somewhat different from total teacher-centered direct instruction. Teachers will need to talk and discuss about the metacognitive journey and encourage peer debate about its strengths and weaknesses. They will need to model metacognitive strategies such as "think-aloud" and encourage students to do it better. They will need to give feedback to students on how they are using metacognitive strategies and perhaps suggest alternatives. They will need to arrange pairs or groups in which peers can give each other feedback about their metacognitive strategies. They need to help move metacognition from the subconscious and implicit to the conscious and explicit, so that students are more in control of it.

Hopefully, by explicating and exemplifying many of the strategies which have been shown to be effective in developing metacognition, teachers have been given clearer ideas about how to actually do this in the classroom.

Reference

Veenman, M. V. J. (2015). Thinking about metacognition improves thinking. In R. Wegerif, L. Li, & J. C. Kaufman (Eds.), *The Routledge International Handbook of Research on Teaching Thinking* (pp. 280–288). London and New York: Routledge.

For Product Safety Concerns and Information please contact our EU representative GPSR@taylorandfrancis.com
Taylor & Francis Verlag GmbH, Kaufingerstraße 24, 80331 München, Germany

www.ingramcontent.com/pod-product-compliance
Lightning Source LLC
Chambersburg PA
CBHW070059020526
44112CB00034B/1732